A guide to observation of scientific phe-
nomena with the magnifying glass—one of
the simplest and easiest of tools.

THROUGH THE MAGNIFYING GLASS

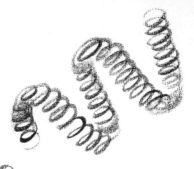

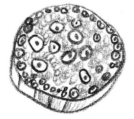

WHITTLESEY HOUSE
McGRAW-HILL BOOK COMPANY
NEW YORK TORONTO LONDON

THROUGH THE MAGNIFYING GLASS

LITTLE THINGS THAT MAKE A BIG DIFFERENCE

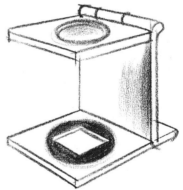

by JULIUS SCHWARTZ

pictures by JEANNE BENDICK

Also by Julius Schwartz

IT'S FUN TO KNOW WHY

Library of Congress Catalog Card Number: 54–6226

Published by Whittlesey House
A division of the McGraw-Hill Book Company, Inc.
Printed in the United States of America

55769

THIRTEENTH PRINTING

To Paul, Alfred, Nicholas,
and to my many other young friends
who joined with me in the search
for the little things.

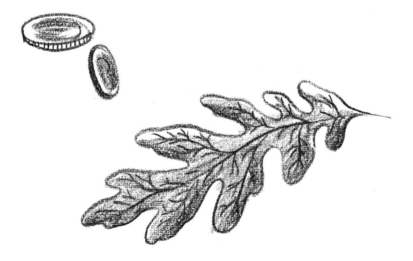

Contents

A New World

THERE IS A NEW WORLD to be discovered on the other side of the magnifying glass. In this world of tiny things there are many curious creatures and wonderful happenings. There you can see

the flashes of exploding atoms

the sparkling of beautiful crystals

the fantastic faces of insects

the cells which nature uses as building blocks

the many-colored dots in magazine pictures

the coils within coils in the filaments of electric bulbs

the craters and ridges of the human skin

the delicate hairs on roots

the pearly eggs of spiders

the hidden letters in a penny

the wriggling waves in phonograph records

These and hundreds of other delights await you when you look at the things around you through a simple magnifying glass. No space ship is needed here; your house and your garden or park have hidden worlds in them for you to explore.

You will do more than look. You will want to know why these small things are built the way that they are. You will want to know how crystals can grow into their perfect shapes. You will want to know why dust can give rise to life. You will want to know how it is possible to tell the age of a fish by the rings on its scales. You will want to know why it is hard to counterfeit a dollar bill.

This book will help you find the answers to these and many other questions. But it will also, we hope, start you on a hobby which will lead you into new worlds not told about here or anywhere.

Lenses and
How to Use Them

All Kinds of Lenses

Now THAT YOU HAVE DECIDED to explore the world of tiny things, you will want to know something about the equipment that you are going to use. Look at the many kinds of magnifying glasses that are used by the men who *must* look closely—by the diamond cutter grinding the 58 sides needed to make a brilliant diamond; by the watchmaker trying to find out what is wrong with your watch; by the printer looking at his type; by the textile woman counting the threads in a piece of cloth; by detectives looking for fingerprints; by secret-service agents looking for counterfeit bills. Lenses are also used by people like yourself, adventuring into the unknown.

WITHOUT SPENDING TOO MUCH MONEY

Magnifying glasses are sold in stationery and department stores, by opticians and scientific supply companies. The prices run from ten cents to ten dollars. Here are a few suggestions for getting lenses without spending too much money. An old box camera whose picture-taking days are over sometimes has good lenses in it. Its picture-taking lens makes a good magnifying glass, and its view finders have more powerful lenses in them. Another place to get lenses is from the companies that sell chipped lenses at low cost. You will find their advertisements in many popular magazines. Your friends and relatives will help you out when they learn that you are making a hobby of peering through lenses. They themselves will be surprised at all the forgotten lenses they find in drawers and boxes.

THE LENS FROM AN OLD
BOX CAMERA IS GOOD

POWER AND LIGHT

The power of the magnifying glasses shown on these pages runs from about three to twenty. Let us be clear about what we mean by "power." When we say that a lens has a magnifying power of eight, for example, we mean that a line that is ⅛ of an inch long will appear to be 1 inch long. All of the things mentioned in this book can be seen with a lens magnifying 10 times, and most of them with less than 10.

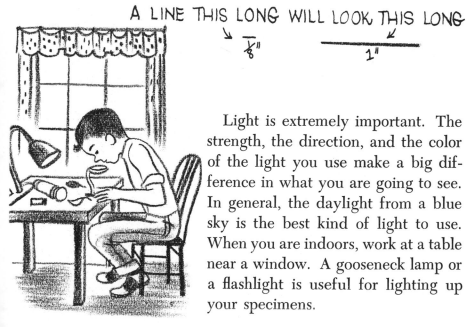

WHEN A LENS HAS
A POWER OF *EIGHT*,

A LINE THIS LONG WILL LOOK THIS LONG
⅛"   1"

Light is extremely important. The strength, the direction, and the color of the light you use make a big difference in what you are going to see. In general, the daylight from a blue sky is the best kind of light to use. When you are indoors, work at a table near a window. A gooseneck lamp or a flashlight is useful for lighting up your specimens.

It is important how this light is used. Some objects look best when they are held between a strong light and you, so that you are looking through them. Others are clearest when held under a strong light, so that their surfaces are lit up. The direction of the light on the object makes a difference. The object changes in appearance as the light is shifted from the front to the back, and from the back to the side.

The background under the object is important. White objects like salt crystals look best on a dark background. Dark objects often look clearest on a light-colored background. Experiment with paper of different shades and colors to get the best results.

WHITE OBJECTS
SHOW UP BEST ON
A DARK BACKGROUND

DARK OBJECTS
LOOK CLEARER
ON A LIGHT
BACKGROUND

Many beautiful colors are brought out in transparent objects when they are looked at with polarized light. This is the special kind of lighting which makes the three-dimensional moving pictures possible. See page 99 for directions on how to use the polarized glasses that are given away at showings of 3-D pictures.

MAKING A VIEWING STAND

It is a good idea to make a viewing stand for yourself. This stand will allow you to look at the specimen that you are studying for a long time without tiring, since it holds the lens for you. At the same time it allows you to use both of your hands for moving the specimen around. All that you need for making this stand is an empty, cleaned milk carton.

IF THE TYPE IS CLEAR AT THIS DISTANCE, FROM HERE TO HERE IS THE FOCUSING DISTANCE

Before you cut the carton to the correct size, you will have to know the focusing distance of your lens. You can find this by looking at some printing, like the words on this page. Move your lens up and down until the print is sharp and clear. Hold the lens in this position and measure the distance between the lens and the page with a ruler. This is the focusing distance.

Measuring from the bottom of the carton up, mark off the focusing distance. Draw a line around the carton at this point, using a ruler to help you. Use a sharp knife or a razor (be careful!) to cut the carton in two, following the lines. The lower part of the carton is going to serve as your viewing stand.

With scissors, cut openings in each of the four sides to within ½ inch of the bottom, as shown in the picture. This operation will leave four strong legs for the viewer. Now cut a square opening in the bottom of the carton, a little bit smaller than your lens. Place your stand on its legs, rest your lens over the opening, and it is ready to be used. If you have a number of

① MARK OFF THE FOCUSING DISTANCE

② CUT CARTON ON YOUR LINE

③ BOTTOM

CUT LEGS LIKE THIS

④ NOW CUT LENS HOLE

LENS

HOLE

lenses with different focusing distances, it is easy to build a separate viewing stand for each.

DELICATE INSTRUMENTS

Magnifying glasses are delicate instruments and should be handled with care. When you are not using your lenses, wrap them separately in tissue and store them in a box. If you carry a lens with you that does not have its own case, make one out of soft cloth or chamois. Magnifying glasses may be cleaned by breathing moisture on them and then wiping them with a soft tissue.

WRITE

As you go along in this magnifying-glass hobby, you will find many of your own special ways of experimenting, and you will see many wonderful things not mentioned in this book. Keep your eyes open and your magnifying glass handy to look at the tiny things around you in your home and garden, in fields and forests, in ponds and streams, in sandy seashores and in rocky ledges. When you find something exciting, write to the author and tell him about it.

KEEP A NOTEBOOK RECORD OF THE INTERESTING THINGS YOU SEE

Right Around You

Skin Deep

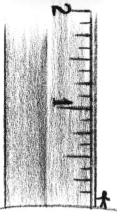

A TINY EXPLORER wandering across the surface of the human skin would find a most interesting landscape: mountain ridges and round craters, grassy jungles and deep pits, pools of salty water and shallow swamps of oil. Peering through the dimly transparent ground, he would see red rivers running below. Walking over these underground rivers, he would feel the ground heaving up and down.

FRICTION RIDGES

With the aid of a magnifying glass, you can explore these wonders of the human skin. Begin with the ridges on your palm and on the underside of your fingers. These fine elevations sweep in different directions over your hands. They are much closer together near your finger tips, where they form a pattern which is all your own. You can read about these in the chapter on Finger-tip Signatures.

BEGIN WITH THE RIDGES HERE

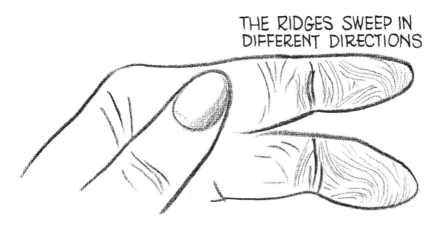

These ridges, which are also found on the soles of your feet, have an important job to do. They prevent slipping by increasing the friction of your hands on anything that they may be grasping, and when you take off your shoes and stockings, they prevent your feet from slipping on the ground. If you notice the direction the ridges take, you will see that they are placed to give the greatest friction. On the first joints of your fingers the ridges sweep in all directions and are very fine. This makes it possible for your hands to do delicate jobs, like threading a needle or holding a tiny jewel.

TWO MILLION CRATERS

The fine ridges of your skin are a good place to look for the sweat pores which open like volcanic craters along these elevations. You can make these craters stand out more clearly if you fill them with a little soot. The best soot for this job is charcoal dust. If you do not have any charcoal around, you can make some by heating a few sticks of clean dry wood (toothpicks will do) in a

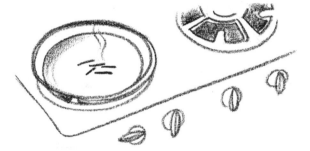

metal pie plate on top of the kitchen range for about five minutes. When the sticks are black, the charcoal is ready to be used.

Make a smudge on a piece of paper with some of this charcoal. Rub the ball of your finger into the charcoal dust. Wipe your finger gently with a piece of cloth to remove any loose charcoal. Now hold your finger under a strong light and look at it with a magnifying glass. At first you will notice that the valleys between the ridges are darkened with charcoal. Looking more carefully, you will see the pores, now blackened with dust, like a row of dots on the spiraling ridges.

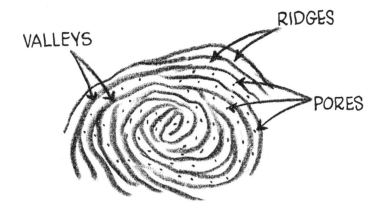

VALLEYS

RIDGES

PORES

Sweat pores are found not only on your hand but all over your body. The entire skin has at least two millions of these tiny openings. Each pore is the outside opening of a tube that goes down into the lower layers of the skin. Here the tube ends in a long coil which looks something like spaghetti. This coil, called a *sweat gland*, takes water and salt from the blood in your skin. This salty water, called sweat or perspiration, then passes up the tube and out through the pores which you just looked at.

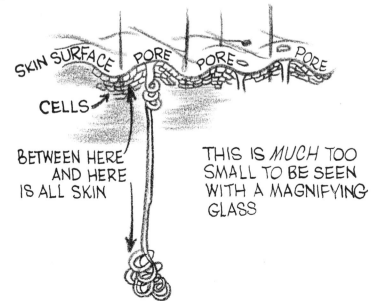

SKIN SURFACE

PORE PORE PORE

CELLS

BETWEEN HERE
AND HERE
IS ALL SKIN

THIS IS *MUCH TOO*
SMALL TO BE SEEN
WITH A MAGNIFYING
GLASS

AN AUTOMATIC HEAT-CONDITIONING SYSTEM

Whether you know it or not, you are perspiring all the time. When you are very active, or when the weather is very hot, the sweat forms little drops on the skin that you can see and feel. At other times the sweat evaporates into the air as quickly as it comes into the pores.

YOU LOSE FROM TWO

TO TEN

GLASSES OF WATER THROUGH YOUR PORES EVERY DAY

In perspiring, your body is doing more than getting rid of the water and the wastes that are in sweat. It is also getting rid of heat. When the sweat evaporates from your pores, it cools your skin, which in turn cools you. Altogether, these openings in your skin, which allow from one to five pints of sweat to leave your body each day, provide you with a wonderful automatic heat-conditioning system.

CRISSCROSSING CREASES

Leave the fine ridges and the craters now and explore the deep valleys, the wrinkles of the skin. First look at the large deep wrinkles on the back of the knuckles. While looking at them, make a fist. Do you see how these wrinkles are stretched out flat and smooth? It is lucky that you have these wrinkles because they allow your skin to stretch easily when you move your fingers, and your arms and legs as well.

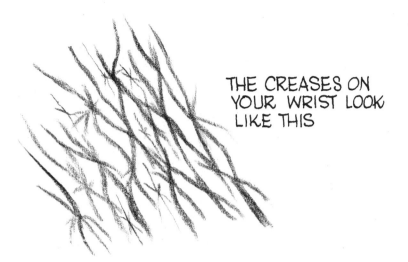

THE CREASES ON
YOUR WRIST LOOK
LIKE THIS

Now move your magnifying glass back to the skin on the upper side of your wrist. What a wonderful network of crisscrossing creases! Here our make-believe explorer would have rough going, leaping from one section of skin to another over these crevices. And, as he hopped up your arm, he would begin to meet the short scattered stalks of hair growing out of the meeting points of these skin creases.

LIKE WHEAT AFTER A RAIN

If you look carefully you will discover that each hair grows out of a tiny hole in your skin. We will talk more about these holes later. In the meantime, notice that all the hairs slant, like wheat after a rain. There are

times, however, when these hairs stand up straight. A sudden chill may have a peculiar effect on the skin, making "goose-pimples" appear. The chill makes tiny muscles in the skin pull each hair into an upright position. At the same time it squeezes the skin into little pimple-like mounds. This goose-pimple action is not of much use to people, but it is important to furry animals. It automatically fluffs up their coats just when they need to be warmer.

BULBS UNDER THE SKIN

Because the skin is partly transparent, you can actually see the part of the hair that is growing under its surface. Look for it with your magnifying glass under a strong light. To get a good look at the rooted part of a hair, be brave and pull a hair out of your scalp, or use a pair of tweezers to remove one from your eyebrow. Under the magnifying glass you will see that the hair ends in a tiny white swelling or bulb. This bulb does the actual growing for the hair, since the part that is above the skin is dead. Will a new hair grow in the hole left where you pulled out a hair? Yes, because at the bottom of the hole there is a living, hair-growing mound of skin which will make a new bulb and a new hair.

OIL FOR A SOFT SKIN

The holes in which the hairs are rooted have another important job to do, which you can discover by running your fingers through your scalp. You will find a fine film of oil left on your fingers. This oil is made by little oil glands under the skin that connect with the hair holes and in that way to the outside. Oil keeps the skin and the hair soft and prevents it from drying out and cracking. Since the leather in our shoes, belts, and handbags is made from the skin of some animal, it is easy to understand why using an oily polish on them will keep them soft and prevent them from cracking.

LIKE AN EVERLASTING PAD

In his journey over your skin, our imaginary explorer would not be touching anything living—because the entire upper layer of the skin is dead. You can see some flakes of this dead skin falling if you rub your scalp and let the pieces fall on a dark cloth. (Many people call these specks of skin *dandruff*, as if it were a sickness. However, this word should be used only when the scalp is losing large amounts of scaly skin.) Skin flakes fall not only from your scalp but from all over your body. It happens when you rub your hands or when you take a bath. How is this dead skin replaced? As the skin wears off on the outside, new living layers are being made underneath. Your skin is like an everlasting pad. As the upper sheets are worn or torn off, new sheets are added below.

A PULSE DETECTOR

Your skin can grow because it is fed by millions of tiny streams of blood that flow through it. You can see the tubes through which some of the larger streams flow on the back of your hand and on your wrist. These tubes, called *veins*, carry blood back to your heart. Buried deeper are the arteries, which carry blood from your heart to the hand. Although you

VEINS AND ARTERIES CARRY BLOOD TO AND FROM YOUR HEART

cannot see the arteries, even with a magnifying glass, there is a most interesting way of finding them with a pulse "detector"—which is going to be an ordinary toothpick!

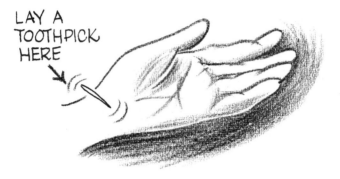

LAY A
TOOTHPICK
HERE

Begin with the artery that doctors feel, the one on your wrist, in line with your thumb. Lay a toothpick down on this spot and watch it. Does it rock up and down like a seesaw? If not, move it around until you find the right spot. The toothpick is acting as a magnifier of the slight up and down movement of the arteries. Each of these movements, called a *pulse beat*, means that your heart has just sent a fresh spurt of blood into your arteries. As the artery in your wrist receives this blood, it swells, pushes against your skin, and rocks your pulse detector. Use the detector and a watch with a second hand to find the number of pulse beats in a minute. Try moving the detector around to find any other arteries buried under your skin.

SKIN DEEP

And so we have seen the many important jobs done by the skin, equipped as it is with skidproof surfaces, heat-conditioning pores, oil-lubricating pits, everlasting pads, and hustling, nourishing blood streams. It has more jobs, acting also as a protecting wall against germs and as a detecting instrument which sends messages telling our brain, "This is smooth," "This is rough," "This is sharp," "This is hot," "This is cold," "This is wet." And all of this happens in a covering that at its thickest is only ⅛ of an inch deep.

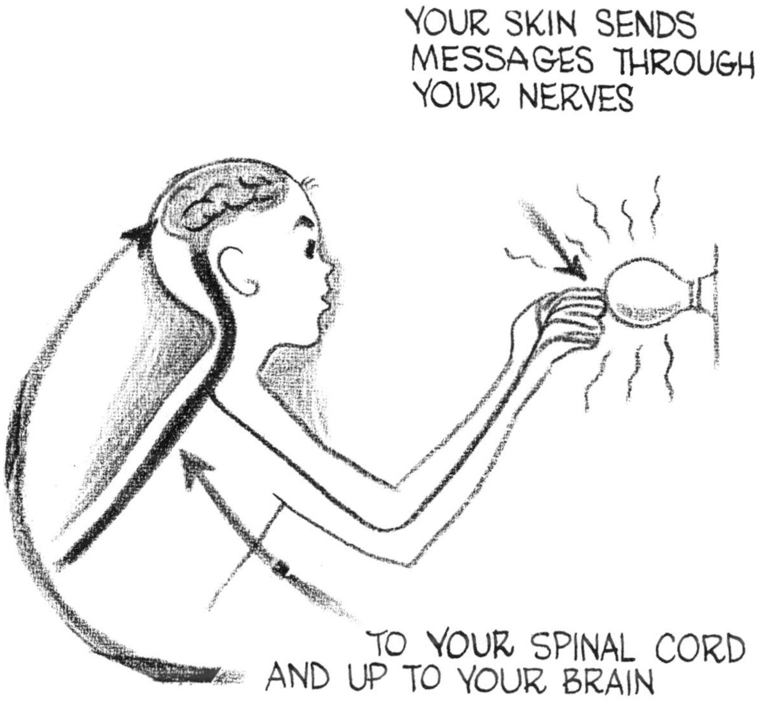

YOUR SKIN SENDS
MESSAGES THROUGH
YOUR NERVES

TO YOUR SPINAL CORD
AND UP TO YOUR BRAIN

Finger-tip Signatures

WHEN YOU SIGN YOUR NAME on a story you have written or a picture you have painted, you are really saying "this is my work." But there is another way of writing your name. It is right on your finger tips.

MAKING A FINGERPRINT

You can get a good look at this finger-tip signature by making a fingerprint. To do this first make an ink pad by folding several layers of cotton material. Place this material in a small dish and pour some ink on it until it is quite damp. Press the first joint of your middle finger on the ink pad. Then press your finger on a clean piece of paper. You may have to repeat this a few times until you get a clear, unsmudged print.

NO TWO ALIKE

This is indeed *your* fingerprint. No other person in the world has a print exactly like it. Now study your fingerprint carefully with a magnifying glass. Notice the many fine lines swirling around to make an interesting design. Make prints of your other fingers. What kind of a design do they make?

WHORL   ARCH   LOOP

WHORLS, ARCHES, AND LOOPS

Although each person has his own special design, fingerprints are alike in some ways. Some fingerprints, for example, form a design called a *whorl*. In this type, the lines circle around each other, as in a target, or they spiral out from the center. Another design is called an *arch*. In this type, the lines go from one side of the print to the other, without curving back. A third kind of design is called a *loop*. In this kind, the lines curve back in a horseshoe turn.

COMPOSITE

Which of these three types does your fingerprint seem to be? Perhaps it is a mixture of arches, loops, and whorls. In that case it is called a *composite*. Whatever your fingerprint pattern is, it remains the same throughout your life. Nothing can change it.

INVISIBLE FINGERPRINTS

All day long you are leaving your fingerprints on everything you touch—on books, dishes, doorknobs, money—even though there is no ink on your fingers. You can prove this to yourself by pressing your finger tips on a clean mirror. The print that you leave there is made by the sweat and oils on your skin. If you look at this print with your magnifying glass, you will see that it has the same swirling lines that you found in the ink fingerprint. This print will remain on the mirror for many days, even weeks, if it is not washed off.

Even a piece of paper that looks perfectly clean may be hiding a fingerprint. This hidden fingerprint can be "developed" so that it can be seen easily. Would you like to develop a fingerprint? Here's how: begin with a clean sheet of paper, fresh from a pad or a notebook. Rub one of your fingers through your hair to make sure that there is enough oil on it. Press this finger on the sheet of paper. To develop the fingerprint you have just left, you will need some ordinary sketching charcoal, a razor blade, and a small wad of absorbent cotton. (If you don't have any charcoal around, see page 22 for directions on how to make some.)

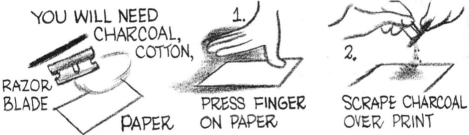

YOU WILL NEED CHARCOAL, COTTON,

RAZOR BLADE

PAPER

1.

PRESS FINGER ON PAPER

2.

SCRAPE CHARCOAL OVER PRINT

Scrape the stick of charcoal with the razor over the part of the paper where you pressed your finger. Do this until the hidden print is covered with charcoal dust. Now tap the paper with a pencil or shake it by its edges so that the charcoal rolls over the fingerprint and sticks to it. Blow all the free charcoal off the paper. You see now the general shape of the print. To make the lines stand out more clearly, dust it very gently with the cotton to remove some of the charcoal. Now you are ready to study the developed print with a magnifying glass.

It might be interesting for you to use your magnifying glass to look for fingerprints that some members of your family may have left on a drinking glass, a mirror, or some other object. To tell *whose* fingerprint you have found, you will first have to make fingerprint records of your whole family, using an ink pad and a piece of paper. Write the name under each fingerprint. Then compare the fingerprint you have found with those on the paper record. Perhaps it is yours!

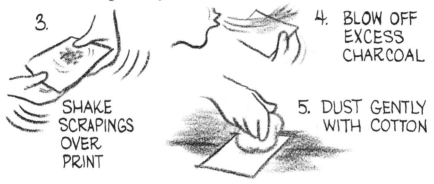

3. SHAKE SCRAPINGS OVER PRINT

4. BLOW OFF EXCESS CHARCOAL

5. DUST GENTLY WITH COTTON

CATCH THE CRIMINAL

Criminals are often caught in the same way that you "caught" the fingerprint maker in your family—because they leave their fingerprints on the things they touch at the place of their crime. When they do this they are signing their name to their bad work. When a detective finds such a fingerprint, he sends a picture of it to the Federal Bureau of Investigation in Washington, D.C. Here the FBI keeps records of the fingerprints of criminals who have been arrested before, together with their names and photographs. An FBI worker looks through the fingerprint records until he finds the one which is exactly like the one sent in. Of course, the FBI man does not have to look through all the millions of fingerprints in the records. He is helped by the fact that fingerprints fall into special groups, like whorls, arches, and loops, as we learned before. He is also helped by a special selecting machine which does part of the work automatically. If he finds the sought-for fingerprint in the records, he sends a report to the inquiring detective, giving the name, the picture, and any other information that the FBI has about the suspected criminal.

But we must not think that only criminals have their fingerprints taken. Men and women in the Armed Forces of the United States, government workers, and thousands of good citizens have their fingerprints in the files of the government. In many hospitals, *footprints* are made of babies a few moments after they are born. These prints, like fingerprints, prevent any possibility of a mix-up of the babies, because no two are alike.

Thousands of years ago honest people used to sign their names to important papers by pressing their fingerprints on a piece of wax which was stuck to the paper. Even at that time they understood that a fingerprint was a way of saying "this is my name, and mine alone."

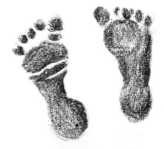

BABY
FOOTPRINTS

Crystal Jewels

JEWEL COLLECTING IS AN EXPENSIVE HOBBY, one that only the rich can afford. There is a kind of jewel collecting, however, that is open to all who are willing to search. The collector need go no further than the pantry shelves or the drug cabinet in his own home to find the jewels that we are talking about—the many-sided crystals of common things. True, these inexpensive jewels are tiny. True, some of them have to be worked on to bring out their natural beauty. But with the help of the magnifying glass and a few easily learned tricks, the collector can soon feast his eyes on a display of glittering gems.

TRICKS OF THE TRADE

There are a few rules that the crystal collector will find useful:

1. Fingers should be kept out of the eyes and mouth while doing these experiments. Hands should be washed when the experiment is over.

EYES AND MOUTH ARE "OUT OF BOUNDS"

WASH HANDS AFTERWARDS

2. Most of the household crystals are colorless or only lightly colored. They will show up best on a dark background.

3. Use a fine paintbrush to pick up single crystals. As you turn the brush you can see the crystal from all sides. A sewing needle is also useful for tumbling the crystals over.

HANDY
HELPERS

FINE BRUSH

NEEDLE

4. When the crystals are too small for easy viewing, or when they are broken, you will want to regrow them. To do this, first dissolve as much as possible of the substance in a quarter of a glass of water. Then pour the clear solution into a smooth-surfaced container like a saucer or an enamel pan. Put it in a place where it will not be disturbed while the water is evaporating. As a rule, the more slowly the water evaporates, the larger the crystals will be.

Instead of pouring the solution into a saucer, you may, if you wish, pour it into a small glass or a vial. If you then hang a string from a toothpick into this solution, larger, more perfect crystals will form on it.

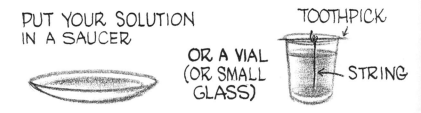

PUT YOUR SOLUTION
IN A SAUCER

OR A VIAL
(OR SMALL
GLASS)

TOOTHPICK

STRING

5. Use polarized light (see page 99) to "paint" your crystals with all the colors of the rainbow.

6. Your neighborhood druggist will be able to supply you with any of the crystal chemicals which you do not have at home. Tell him what you want to use them for. Ask him for small quantities.

DISAPPEAR—REAPPEAR

Begin with some ordinary table salt. The magnifying glass shows us that it is not a powder; rather it is made of tiny gleaming cubes. Add a drop of water to a few of these crystals. Under the lens you will see the cubes become smaller and smaller as they dissolve and disappear into the water. Soon there is no sign of the salt. The crystals have separated into such tiny particles that they cannot be seen, even with the most powerful microscopes.

TABLE SALT CUBES
(YOU WILL SEE THEM
BEST AGAINST A
DARK BACKGROUND)

These scattered particles can come together again and grow into even larger crystals than the ones you started

STIR 2 TEASPOONS OF
SALT

INTO $\frac{1}{2}$ GLASS OF WATER

THEN POUR INTO A SOUP PLATE

SOME CUBES MIGHT LOOK LIKE THIS

with. To see this happen, start all over again by stirring two teaspoons of salt into one-half of a glass of warm water. Pour the clear liquid into a soup plate or an enamel pan to the height of about one-eighth of an inch. Allow the water to evaporate in the sunlight or in a warm place. This may take a day or two but you will be rewarded by the sight of the large crystals. Some of these crystals take on a special shape, looking as if each side of the cube had been hollowed out in the form of a pyramid.

ATOMS WITH RULES

Why does salt crystallize in the form of a cube? First we must understand that the salt you dissolved in the water was made of billions of tiny invisible particles called atoms. These atoms are of two kinds, one called sodium and the other called chlorine. (Perhaps you can understand now why the chemist calls salt *sodium chloride.*) These atoms were scattered in the water. As the water evaporated the atoms came closer together to form little groups. But these are not helter-skelter groups. The atoms seem to follow certain rules:

1. Each chlorine atom must be near sodium atoms.
2. Each sodium atom must be near chlorine atoms.
3. All the atoms are the same distance from each other.

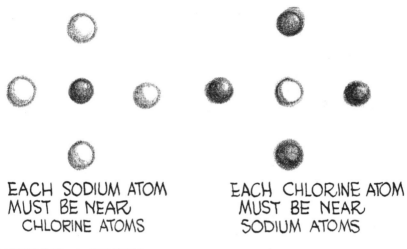

EACH SODIUM ATOM
MUST BE NEAR
CHLORINE ATOMS

EACH CHLORINE ATOM
MUST BE NEAR
SODIUM ATOMS

MODELING A CRYSTAL

But to understand these rules best, build your own model of a salt crystal. All you need is modeling clay of two colors (red and blue, for example) and a box of toothpicks. Roll the clay to make 14 red and 14 blue balls, each about three-quarters of an inch across. The red balls will be the "sodium atoms" and the blue ones the "chlorine atoms." The toothpicks will be used to hold the clay balls together. In a real crystal, there is really nothing like a toothpick. The atoms are held together by a mysterious attraction which scientists do not fully understand. So, if we must give the toothpicks a name, it should be "atomic attraction."

Now begin to build the model of the salt crystal, following the crystal-building rules. Your completed model is made of 27 atoms (one is left over), which form a perfect cube. If you have a great deal of patience and plenty of clay and toothpicks you can add to this atomic house by following the same rules. You will find that it grows into a larger structure, but it is still a cube.

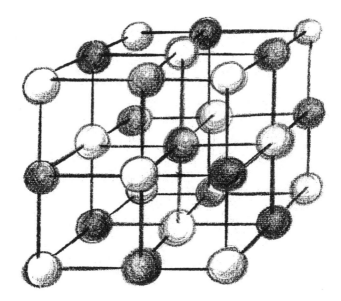

Real salt crystals grow as your model did, by the piling on of atoms according to the rules of the game. But only when billions of atoms have been attracted together is it large enough for you to see it as a crystal of salt.

PLAYING WITH DIFFERENT RULES

So we see that the shape that a salt crystal takes depends on the way in which its atoms arrange themselves. Other chemicals have differently shaped crystals because their atoms play the attraction game with different rules. Look, for example, at some of the crystals of Epsom salts which may be in your medicine chest. Our

eyes show us that these crystals are long and thin. Tumbling them around with a needle, while looking at them under a magnifying glass, we discover that the crystals have four long flat sides as shown in the picture. The ends are like pitched roofs but each is set differently on the sides.

Turning now to the house-cleaning department, we find that some products which are advertised to clean walls and woodwork have long crystals in them. Pushing these around under the lens we find that they have six long sides, but flat "roofs." It would seem that these cleaners all have the same chemical in them, known as *trisodium phosphate.*

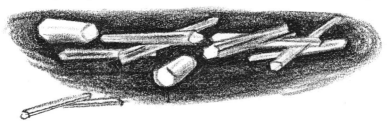

Borax, also a washing aid, and alum, from your drug shelf, will make large crystals if they are first dissolved in water and then allowed to stand in flat dishes or enamel trays. In both cases use polarized light (see page 99) to see the crystal faces in many beautiful colors. Borax forms complicated, many-sided crystals, while alum forms eight-sided crystals.

YOU CAN
MINE
CRYSTALS
HERE

If you allow some tincture of iodine to evaporate on a piece of glass, it will leave many pretty crystals of different sizes, but all quite small. You will find larger crystals forming where the drying is slowest. Blue vitriol, which you can buy in your neighborhood drugstore, forms beautiful blue crystals when it evaporates from a water solution. These are wonderful to look at under polarized light.

CRYSTALS FROM THE SKY

But the most magnificent crystals of all are the snowflakes, made in the great outdoor laboratory of the sky. Mr. W. A. Bentley was so fascinated with the many beautiful designs of snowflakes that he spent a good many years of his life photographing them. He moved his camera into snowstorms to make everlasting pictures of these fleeting crystals. The drawings on this page are copied from his original photographs.

To see snow crystals, wait for a fall of small dry flakes. Chill a piece of dark cloth, like velvet, and the magnifying glass that you are going to use by placing them in your refrigerator for about half an hour. Catch a few flakes on the cloth and then study them in a sheltered place out of doors. Don't breathe too hard on the flakes or they will disappear.

Probably no one before you has seen the same designs that you are looking at now. However, practically all snow crystals are built on a six-sided plan.

NATURE'S SHOWCASE

These, then, are the crystals that we find in the common things around us. If we wish to go further in our search, we should turn to the large chemical laboratories of the earth itself to find in its rocks the large, beautiful mineral crystals. Here, as in our little home laboratories, atoms join together to form the glittering, polished gems of nature's showcase.

Splitting Atoms

You ARE LIVING at the opening of a new age—the atomic age. Man has learned the secrets of the atom. He can split these tiny particles to make them give up their stored power.

But for billions of years certain kinds of atoms have been splitting by themselves, without any help from man. The tiny explosions caused by these atoms went unnoticed until about fifty years ago, when the self-exploding atoms of radium and uranium were discovered.

ATOMS SPLITTING IN YOUR WRIST WATCH

Would you like to see the flashes caused by self-exploding atoms? All you need is a watch (or a clock) with a luminous dial, a magnifying glass, and a darkened room. The magnifying glass should be a strong one. To test its strength, hold it close to your eye and bring your finger

IF YOUR FINGER IS IN FOCUS AT A DISTANCE OF 1" OR LESS, YOUR GLASS IS RIGHT FOR ATOM DETECTING

into clear focus. If the distance between the lens and your finger is now about one inch or less, then it is suited for the atom-detecting job.

The dial of the watch should be the kind that glows all night. Other cheaper types, which glow only for a short time after the lights are turned off, will not do.

The best time to see the atomic flashes is at night. Turn the lights out and wait at least ten minutes for your eyes to become accustomed to the darkness. While you are waiting, look at the dial of the watch (without using the magnifying glass) to see the soft glow becoming brighter and brighter.

Now you are ready to take a close look. Hold the magnifying glass near your eye. Move the watch back and forth until its dial is clear—in sharp focus. Look steadily at the dial for a few minutes. No longer do you see a quiet glow. Instead there is a shimmering light, a sparkling from many points on the dial, like flashing stars.

The soft glow that you saw before is really made by these many sparkling points. What caused these flashes?

A TARGET FOR SPLITTING ATOMS

To answer this question, let us first think about the paint which the watch manufacturer uses to make the hands and the numbers of the watch glow in the dark. In this paint there is mixed a small amount of self-splitting atoms. In most watches these are the atoms of a chemical called *radiothorium*. As the radiothorium atoms split, small particles are shot out of them. However, these atomic bullets by themselves would not light up your watch. They are something like the bullets shot out of rifles at the sideshows in fairs and carnivals. You can't see the bullets fly through the air, but you know that one did when it hits a target to make a "bong."

WHEN A PART OF THE SPLITTING ATOM   HITS THE ZINC SULFIDE, THERE'S A FLASH

To make a target for the self-splitting atoms, the manufacturer mixes a second chemical in the paint, something called *zinc sulfide*. Every time an atomic bullet hits this chemical there is a flash. This means that each flash that you see is made by the explosion of one atom.

BILLIONS OF ATOMS—BILLIONS OF YEARS

Every second, day and night, dozens of atoms in your watch are splitting. Once having split, these particular atoms cannot split again. Then how can your watch continue to glow year after year? The answer is that there are billions of radiothorium atoms in your watch's dial. Scientists figure that only half of these atoms will have split in twenty billion years.

ATOMIC POWER FOR SPACE SHIPS

In your watch only a few atoms are splitting each second. Recently, man has learned how to make billions of atoms split in a single second to release their combined power at the same moment. This atomic power is enormous. The atomic splitting of one pound of uranium atoms makes as much power as the burning of two and one-half million pounds of coal.

With this atomic power, we will be able, one day soon, to run planes and ships, heating plants and electric generators. With this new power we will be able to replace our fast decreasing supply of coal and oil. In your lifetime, perhaps, this mighty power will make it possible for us to send ships into space to explore the moon and other heavenly bodies.

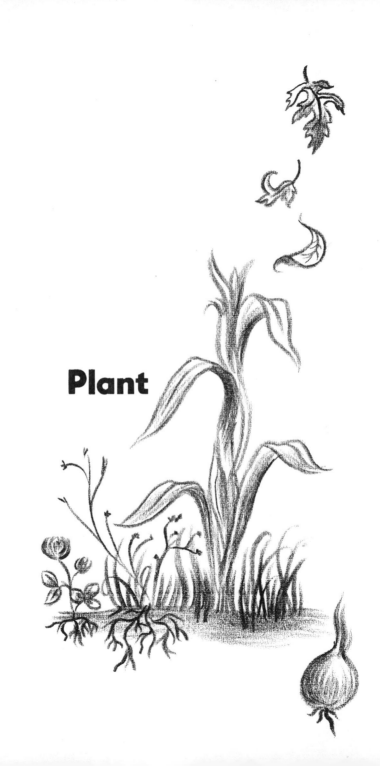

Plant

51

The Onion and You

WHEN WE THINK OF ONIONS, we usually think of the steaks and hamburgers which often go with them. Or perhaps we remember the tears which raw onions bring to our eyes. But the ordinary onion can bring delights to our eyes as well—when seen through the magic of the magnifying glass. For in the magnified onion we can discover something which is found in trees, in elephants, in you—in all living things.

DRY AND DYE

Get a big onion, the bigger the better. Shop around until you find one that is four or five inches across its middle. With a sharp knife, cut the onion through its center into top and bottom halves. Then cut a ¼-inch slice from one of the halves—just the size that you might want for a hamburger sandwich.

CUT SLICE FROM HERE

Place the slice of onion on a plate and let it dry for about an hour. Drying does two useful things. It allows the tear-making juices to escape from the cut surface of the onion. At the same time, drying makes magnifying-glass study easier, because when the glistening, reflecting juices evaporate they leave the underlying surface clearer.

Now examine the cut slab of onion with your magnifying glass, preferably one of eight power or more. Do you begin to see many bubblelike structures? You will be able to see them more clearly if you brush a little blue ink over the onion with a matchstick or a paintbrush. Allow the ink to dry for a few minutes. Now examine the dried and dyed onion under a strong light.

YOU CAN STUDY YOUR ONION UNDER A LIGHT   OR OVER IT

WHAT MAKES AN ONION AN ONION?

The whole onion seems to be made of thousands of these "bubbles" or *cells*, as they are called. Wherever you look with your magnifying glass you see cells, each with a blue-stained wall around it. These cells are not all the same size. Those near the outside of the onion are larger than those near the center. Can you guess why? The cells near the center are young, recently made cells. Those near the outer edge are older and have had more time to grow.

Onion cells can grow because they are alive. And because they grow, the whole onion grows. Indeed, all these thousands and millions of cells together make the onion an onion. They make it grow the way it does, taste the way it does, smell the way it does.

And what is true for the onion is true for all living things. We have chosen the onion only because its cells are large and because it is easy to get. But apple trees and grasses, elephants and crickets, and you, are made of these tiny cells of life.

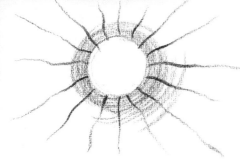

Pipes in Plants

Plants are busy, bustling factories. Roots, growing and digging, mine the soil for its precious minerals and water. Leaves, spreading their greenness to the sun, trap its rays to manufacture sugar. And stems, joining the underground roots to the leaves on high, are filled with many moving streams.

A PLUMBING SYSTEM OF MANY PIPES

These streams move up and down in a plumbing system of many pipes: pipes which carry soil water from the roots up to the leaves, pipes which carry food from the leaves down to the stem and roots.

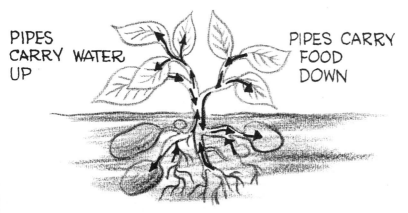

PIPES CARRY WATER UP

PIPES CARRY FOOD DOWN

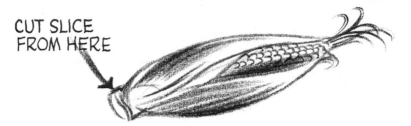

CUT SLICE
FROM HERE

Let us look for these pipes in the stem of a corn plant. No, you don't have to go to a cornfield. Instead, you can use the small stem that is left on an ear of fresh corn, which you can buy in your neighborhood store. Cut a piece about half an inch long from the end of this stem. Allow it to dry for about half an hour. Then stain the cut end of this stem with some ordinary blue ink. Do this by placing a small drop of ink in the center and spreading it thin with your finger. Allow it to dry for a minute or two.

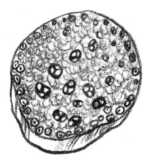

Notice that the ink does not stain the cut corn stem evenly. It brings out a number of dark blue dots. Look at these dots more carefully under a strong light, using your magnifying glass. Also try cutting a thin slice off the stained stem, using a single-edged razor blade. (Be careful! Don't slice your fingers!) Then look *through* it, holding it over a strong light. Either way it is a beautiful sight. The dots that you saw before have now been magnified into curious tiny "faces," each with two large "eyes" and some with a "mouth." Notice the many small "faces" near the edge and the larger ones scattered across the stem.

BUNDLES

Each of these "faces" is made of a number of different kinds of pipes. What we called the "eyes" and the "mouth" are really the cut ends of some of the larger pipes. There are many smaller ones, too small for you to see with a magnifying glass. A collection of pipes that forms such curious "faces" in the corn plant is called a *bundle*.

Some of the pipes in each bundle carry materials up, and some of them carry materials down the corn stem. If you would like to see pipes like these in their *length* make a cut through a piece of stained corn stem the long way. The straight, colored lines that you see are the bundles.

BUNDLES

A RED TRACER

How would you like to see these pipes doing one of their jobs—carrying water up a stem? To see this you will need a fresh celery stalk. Cut off the lower ½ inch from a celery stalk. Save this small piece because you are going to study it later. Stand the celery stalk, cut end down, in a jar containing about half an inch of red ink. Allow it to stand there for several hours.

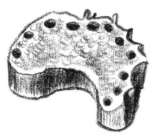

Let the small piece you cut from the bottom of the stalk dry for about half an hour. Then smear a little ink on the cut surface. Study it with your magnifying glass. This time, instead of a sea of faces, you see a crescent containing about a dozen "eyes," each with an "eyebrow," set in a network of surrounding cells. Each of these "eyes" is, of course, a bundle of water- and food-carrying pipes.

Now return to your celery stalk, which has been in ink for several hours. Can you see the long bundles of the celery traced in red? Take the celery out of the ink so that you can study it more closely. Wipe the extra ink off with a piece of paper toweling. Look at the cut edge at the bottom of the stalk to see the bundles, stained a deep red, and the surrounding cells, also

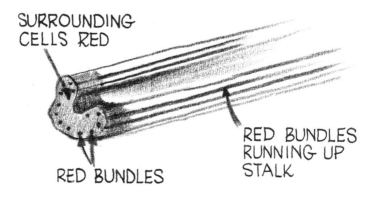

SURROUNDING
CELLS RED

RED BUNDLES
RUNNING UP
STALK

RED BUNDLES

stained red. Now begin making thin ⅛-inch slices of the stalk every inch or so, working your way up the stem and into the leaves. Hold these slices over a strong light and look at them with your magnifying glass. Do you see that the bundles are stained red, while the surrounding cells are not? This shows that it is the bundles that are doing the job of carrying liquids up the stalk. To see these bundles in their length, cut through a 1-inch piece of celery the long way.

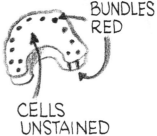

BUNDLES RED

CELLS UNSTAINED

The red ink has acted as a "tracer," showing you clearly its pathway up the stalk and into the leaves of the celery. Tracer methods like these are used by scientists when they wish to follow the path of different chemicals in living things. Recently they have

been using atomic tracers. When these are put inside a plant or an animal, they give off atomic radiations. These radiations cannot be seen by the eye. Instead they are detected by a Geiger counter, a machine which counts click . . . click . . . click slowly when the radiations are weak, but goes clickclickclickclickclickclick quickly when the radiations are strong. Using this atomic-tracer method, scientists are discovering many secrets hidden in plants and animals.

GEIGER COUNTER

PIPES IN LEAVES

All of us have seen pipe bundles in leaves—only we know them as *veins*. These veins are connected directly to the bundles that start in the roots and go up the stems to enter the leaves. Here they are easy to see because leaves are thin and translucent. Use your magnifying glass to study the veins of different kinds of leaves. In corn, grass, and lily leaves see how the main veins run side by side in the same direction. You may use the green husk around your ear of corn to see this kind of veining. See also how these large veins are connected by smaller ones. In other kinds of leaves, like oak, maple, lilac, and ivy, the veins branch and divide into smaller and smaller veins. You can see this type in the leaf of the celery plant. In both kinds of leaves, the veins branch to reach every part of the leaf.

Within these veins are the pipes which bring to the leaf factories the raw materials for their sugar-manufacturing cells. Within these veins also are the pipes which carry sugar from the cells where it is made to the stems and roots and, at times, to the seeds and fruits of these busy, bustling plants.

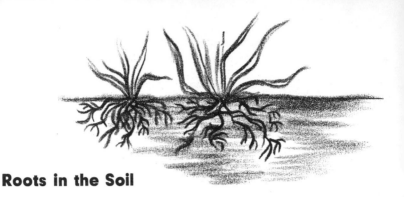

Roots in the Soil

How BIG ARE THE ROOTS of a plant? One scientist tried to find out by studying a single plant of winter rye grass. He grew this plant by itself in a wooden box filled with rich soil. The box was one foot square at the top and was about two feet deep.

At the end of four months the plant had grown to a height of twenty inches. The scientist then washed all the soil out of the box and measured the roots carefully. From his measurements he figured out that if all the roots were spread flat, they would cover about seven thousand square feet—enough to completely cover two and a half tennis courts! How could the roots in this small boxful of earth cover such a large surface?

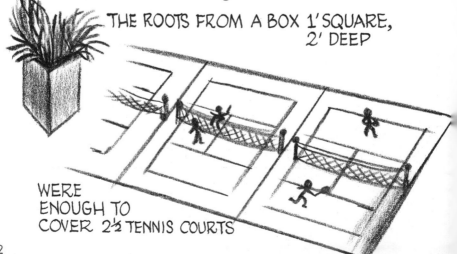

THE ROOTS FROM A BOX 1' SQUARE, 2' DEEP

WERE ENOUGH TO COVER 2½ TENNIS COURTS

HAIRS ON ROOTS

If you have ever seen a small up-rooted tree, or if you have ever pulled a small plant out of the soil with its roots, you know part of the answer. The root branches again and again into thousands of small rootlets. All this you can see. But what you do not usually see are the billions of tiny root hairs which bring the plant into such close touch with the soil.

You can see these root hairs clearly by growing some plants without using soil. To do this you will need a covered dish, a blotter, water, and some seeds. The plastic container that many cheeses come in nowadays can serve as your covered dish. Radish seeds are good to use because they are easy to get and quick to sprout. However, you can also use quick-sprouting seeds like beans, peas, corn, wheat, oats, and squash.

Cut the blotter to fit the bottom of the dish, wet it, and then shake all the extra water out of it before putting it on the bottom of the container. Scatter ten or fifteen radish seeds on the moist blotter, cover the dish, and keep it in a warm place, a closet, perhaps.

1. PUT WET BLOTTER IN BOTTOM OF DISH

2. SCATTER SEEDS ON BLOTTER

3. COVER AND KEEP IN A WARM PLACE

1.

2.

3.

4.

5.

BEGINNING OF
ROOT HAIRS

ROOT
6.   HAIRS
ROOT

SHELL

Since the seeds sprout at different speeds, you will find them in different stages of growth any day that you study them. One or two days after the "planting," you will probably find that some seeds have not changed in their appearance except that they are larger than the small dry ones you began with. Others have just begun to show a crack in their hard brown coats, with a bright yellow root pushing its way out. In other seeds the little fat root has poked its way out of the shell and has grown a pointed tip into the blotter. Some seeds have gone farther than this, having also pushed out green leafy parts from the brown shell. And on one or two of the pointed roots you may see what at first looks like a swelling. On closer inspection with a magnifying glass you discover that this swelling is really a coat of hundreds of delicate white hairs. These are the root hairs.

7.   BEGINNING OF
GREEN LEAVES

A HAIR 6,000 MILES LONG

A day or so later all of the roots of the seedlings are covered with this white, cottony fuzz. How would you like to count all the root hairs on a single seedling? That would be a very hard job indeed. Yet the scientist whom we were talking about before did a job like this on his rye-grass plant. He found that there were 14 billion of them! There were six times as many root hairs on this one little plant as there are people on the whole earth. He also figured that if all these hairs were attached end to end to make a single hair, they would reach from New York to San Francisco and back again, a distance of about 6,000 miles.

These miles of root hairs are working for the plant, pushing their thin walls into close contact with billions of soil particles and taking in precious minerals and water. A plant's life depends on these billions of hairs. That is why we must be careful not to rip off these tiny roots when we dig up and move a tree or any other growing plant to a new place. In transplanting a tree, we dig around and under the roots, and then lift it with the soil from underneath.

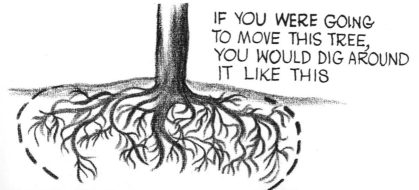

IF YOU WERE GOING TO MOVE THIS TREE, YOU WOULD DIG AROUND IT LIKE THIS

GRASS ROOTS

You have just seen some roots in the protected privacy of your little blotter-dish garden. Now take a look at a fully grown root in its natural home—the soil. To do this, dig out a small clump of grass. Shake some of the soil out of the clump to see a few of the roots clearly. Hold one of these up to the light and look at it with your magnifying glass. Do you see the wavy roots and their tiny rootlets? See also how small bits of soil stick to the zigzagging roots. If you wish to see the roots more clearly, dip the clump into a pail of water to wash away the soil.

BITS OF SOIL CLING
TO THE ROOTS

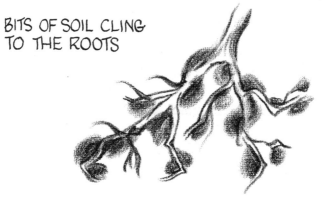

Notice how much soil was held by those twining roots! It took quite a bit of shaking and washing to get it off. This tight grip that the roots of grasses and other plants have on the soil is important in protecting its open surface. It prevents water from washing the topsoil away, and it prevents wind from blowing it away.

But man himself has done a great deal of damage to this precious soil cover. He harvests his crop of corn, leaving his fields bare and unprotected. The soil, no longer gripped by the network of tangled roots, is easily blown or washed away. He can avoid this by planting "cover" crops, that is, by growing a new crop of plants after the harvest. This cover crop holds the soil through the fall, the winter, and the early spring.

A STRANGE PARTNERSHIP

High on the list of man's plant friends is clover. There is a special reason for this which you can discover if you take the trouble to take a close look at its roots. To do this dig up a clump of ordinary clover. From the cluster, separate out one plant with its leaves, stem, and roots. Wash the roots thoroughly to get rid of all the soil.

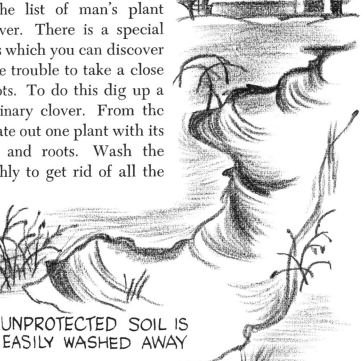

UNPROTECTED SOIL IS
EASILY WASHED AWAY

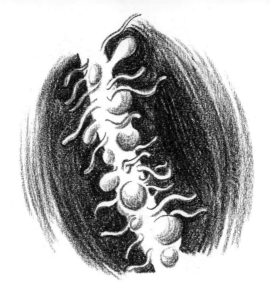

On this occasion, you are going to feel something before you see it. Draw one of the cleaned roots between two of your fingers. Do you feel little bumps as you do this? Try to find what these bumps are by looking at the root with a magnifying glass. There you will see a number of round swellings of different sizes attached to the roots. There may be as many as a dozen of these swellings for every inch of root. What are these swellings? How did they get there?

When the clover plant is very young, living bacteria from the soil work their way into its roots. They make their home there, feeding and multiplying. The roots of the clover plant grow little swellings around each of these colonies of bacteria. These swellings, called *nodules,* are the ones that you felt and saw before. Each of them is filled with millions of bacteria. Your lens cannot show you these bacteria, but a thousand-powered microscope can.

These swellings are good for the plant! In return for the protection and the nourishment they get, the nodule bacteria manufacture for the plant an important chemical called nitrate. Nitrates are needed by clover and by all plants for their strength and their growth.

The wise farmer knows this. That is why he plants clover every few years in his wheat field. That is why he plows the full-grown clover right back into the soil. For he knows that the clover will put back into the soil the nitrates which the harvested wheat took from it. The farmer is profiting from the strange partnership of clover and bacteria.

Flowers at Work

MANY DELIGHTFUL SURPRISES AWAIT you when you turn your magnifying glass on the world of flowers. Find some high grass growing in a field or along a roadside. On its feathery plumes or slender spikes the magnifying glass reveals hundreds of tiny flowers. These odd-shaped flowers, without petals, are delicately tinted in yellow, lavender, white, or purple. Small as they are, they can fill a whole field with color.

Under the magnifying glass, the common red-clover "flower" becomes a cluster of dozens of pealike blossoms—a bouquet in miniature. Other tiny flowers that are neglected by most of us are those of the trees. While most of us are familiar with the showy blossoms of the dogwoods, the magnolias, and the fruit trees, very few of us have discovered the hidden beauty of the tiny blossoms of the maples, the elms, and the oaks.

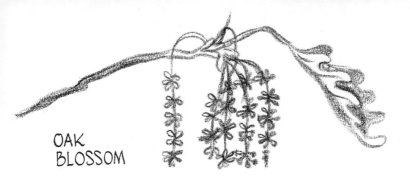

OAK
BLOSSOM

Tiny or large, flowers have two important kinds of structures within them, the *stamens* and the *pistils*. These parts are important because they work together to make the seeds of the plant. The many stamens, topped with a yellow, dustlike powder, are more familiar to us. They surround the one or more pistils, which are usually placed near the center of the flower.

But to be at home with all the members of the family of flowers, you must first become acquainted with one. For this, it is better to select a large flower, so that you can handle it easily and see its parts clearly. We have chosen such a flower, the day lily, but any flower that you find convenient will do for this acquaintanceship.

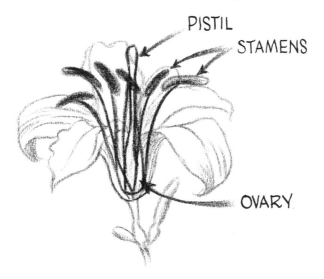

PISTIL

STAMENS

OVARY

ANTHERS THAT TURN INSIDE OUT

Leaving the attractively colored petals, let us turn to the parts of the flower which have the important tasks of pollen making and seed making. Pollen making is the job of the six slender stamens. Each of these has a curved stem topped with a yellow-brown anther. Turn your lens on one of these anthers. This boat-shaped

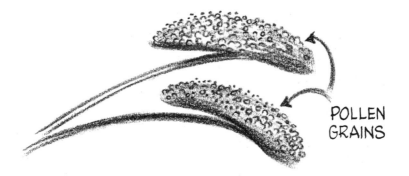

POLLEN GRAINS

structure is loaded with many hundreds of tiny yellow grains. To see each of these grains, which are called *pollen*, more clearly, dip an anther into some water in a shallow glass dish. Place the dish on a dark background and examine it under a bright light.

It is interesting to see how a young anther ripens until it reaches the state where it is bursting with pollen. To see this, find some unopened flower buds. If you open such a bud in the day lily, you will find that the anthers are covered with a purplish-brown coat, but

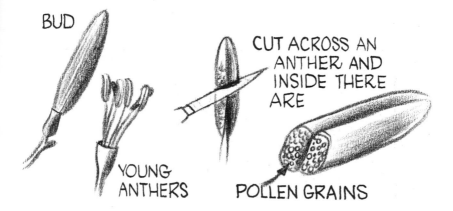

BUD

YOUNG ANTHERS

CUT ACROSS AN ANTHER AND INSIDE THERE ARE

POLLEN GRAINS

there is no sign of pollen grains. Where are they? To find them, cut across an anther with a sharp knife and look at the cut with your magnifying glass. You find that the anther is made of two tubes, each packed with pollen grains. How do these grains get to the outside of the anther?

To find out, take another young stamen and hold its unopened anther over something hot, like a lighted match or an electric bulb, for a minute. You will see the anther's purple coat splitting open on both sides. As it splits, it curls so that the inside of the anther is twisted to the outside, bringing the yellow pollen grains out into the open. Slowly but surely the anther has turned itself inside out.

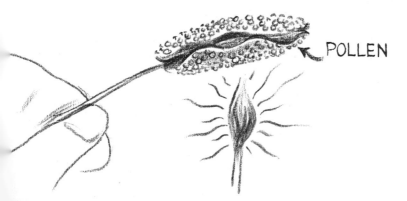

POLLEN

The same kind of thing happens naturally in a lily flower. The heat of summer makes the anthers dry out and split, pushing the thousands of pollen grains into a position where they can be carried away. But to see what happens to the pollen, let us first take a look at the other important part of the flower—the pistil.

A WHITE CROWN TURNS TO GOLD

The pistil's job is to make seeds. The day lily has just one pistil. You can recognize it because it is longer than the stamens and because it is not topped with an anther. Look at its upper tip with a lens to see its small crown of white threads. What does this crown do? You can discover this for yourself by touching a ripe anther to the white crown of the pistil. It is as if you had touched it with a magic wand—the white crown turns to gold. Under the lens, you see dozens of yellow pollen grains caught on the sticky white threads.

IF YOU TOUCH THE WHITE CROWN WITH A RIPE ANTHER, THE POLLEN STICKS, AND IT TURNS TO GOLD

A POLLEN TUBE MUST ENTER

The job, then, of the pistil crown is to catch and hold any pollen grains that might be brought there by wind or by insects. The pollen grains are needed to help the pistil in its job of making seeds. First, the pollen grains must grow long thin tubes from the crown of the pistil down to the swelling at its bottom. We cannot see the pollen tubes growing without the help of a microscope, but we can see how the swelling, called the *ovary*, is preparing itself for its part in seed making.

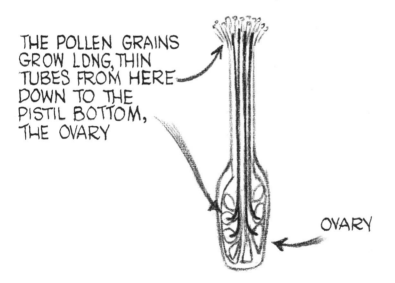

THE POLLEN GRAINS GROW LONG, THIN TUBES FROM HERE DOWN TO THE PISTIL BOTTOM, THE OVARY

OVARY

Remove the petals from the flower. Then carefully slit the slender cup to which the petals were attached. You have now laid bare the green, swollen ovary. Cut across it with a sharp knife or a razor. (Careful!) Under the

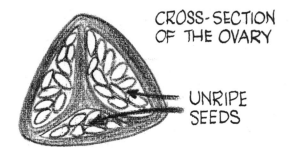

CROSS-SECTION OF THE OVARY

UNRIPE SEEDS

lens it looks something like a miniature cucumber, green and juicy. The ovary is divided into three parts, each filled with pearly white beads. These are the unripe seeds. But before they can ripen, a pollen tube must enter each of them.

TO MAKE THE NEXT GENERATION

Pistils and stamens—these are the important parts of flowers. Look for them in various flowers to see the differences in their shapes and sizes, their colors and their positions, and in their numbers. Look also to see how these pollen-making and seed-making structures are preparing for the next generation. And don't forget to use your magnifying glass to help you in your adventures into flowerland.

Life in Dust

Is THERE LIFE IN DUST? There is no sign of it when you look at dust through the magnifying glass. You can see grains of various sizes and colors, threads and hairs, sand and soot—but no sign of life. Yet from some of these scattered, shapeless specks, life can rise.

For in this dust are the spores—the "seeds"—of those simple plants called *molds*. These dry, hard-shelled specks are quiet, asleep. They are waiting for the right conditions to burst out of their shells and to become active, growing plants.

A DISH-AND-PAPER GARDEN

You can easily give the mold spores the conditions that they need for their growth by making a dish-and-paper garden for them. First get a dish with a cover. The flat plastic cheese container you used for studying root hairs is excellent because you can peep through its transparent walls to see how your garden is growing.

Your plants will need water. To provide this, cut a piece of paper toweling to fit the bottom of the dish. Wet the paper and then pour all the extra water out. As the days go by, be sure to keep the paper damp (not soaking wet) so that your plants get enough water. Keep your dish garden closed so that the water does not evaporate from it too quickly.

1. CUT PAPER TOWELING TO FIT THE DISH. KEEP IT QUITE DAMP.

2. TOUCH A SMALL SQUARE OF BREAD TO A DUSTY PLACE, PUT IT, DUST SIDE UP ON THE DAMP PAPER

Your plants will need food. Bread is good because the particular kind of mold that we are interested in grows best on bread. Cut a small piece, about one inch square, and touch it to a dusty floor to pick up the invisible mold spores. Then place the bread, dusty side up, on the moistened paper toweling. Close the dish and keep it in a dark, warm place like a closet or a drawer.

3. KEEP THE CLOSED DISH IN A DARK, WARM PLACE

LIKE A BALLOON ON A STRING

You have given the sleeping specks of life four of the important things that they need for growth—water, food, darkness, and warmth. Look at your dish every day to see what is happening. Lift the lid and search carefully with your magnifying glass. For a few days you will see no change. But one morning you will find that a white cottony growth has appeared on the bread. The invisible spores in the dust have grown into a mass of living white threads. Some of these threads have spread from the bread to the paper toweling. Here it is easier to see and study them. You will also find it convenient at times to lift the entire growth with the paper out of the dish.

UNDER THE SURFACE ARE
RUNNERS LIKE THIS

If you study the growth carefully with a magnifying glass, you will find that it is more than a cottony tangle. Taking a really close look, you will see that some of the threads grow away from the rest and rise up into the air. On top of some of these there is a tiny white ball, looking like a balloon on a string. On other threads the

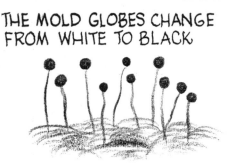

THE MOLD GLOBES CHANGE FROM WHITE TO BLACK

EACH BLACK GLOBE IS PACKED WITH NEW SPORES

(YOU NEED A MICROSCOPE TO SEE THEM)

balls are black. In a day or so your whole mold garden is full of these black globes. To the eye, the mold has changed from a white to a gray-black color. What is the meaning of all of this?

The mold plants are now ripe. Each of these black globes is packed with thousands of tiny new spores. When the globes burst open, the spores will scatter to become part of the billions of specks of dust in the air. Each of these spores can start a new growth of mold, if it has the right conditions.

TO FIGHT AGAINST DISEASE

Perhaps molds of different colors are growing in your garden—yellow, pink, orange, and brown. Each of these colors is made by the different kinds of mold plants that may be growing there. Very often, the growth of the black bread mold, like the kind which you have just studied, is followed by a green mold. Most likely this green mold is the now well-known Penicillium. From this plant man has been able to get a wonderful drug in his fight against disease—penicillin.

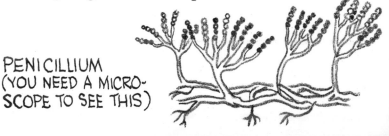

PENICILLIUM (YOU NEED A MICRO-SCOPE TO SEE THIS)

Animal

Sap on Legs

"INSECTS FROM MARS!" That is what one young person said when he looked at the colony of curious creatures which had made their home on a goldenrod leaf. For these aphids, or plant lice, are indeed strange-looking insects. As your eye sweeps over their little world, you wonder if they are really alive. They are so motionless you feel that you are looking at a wax exhibit in a museum. As you look carefully at just a few, you begin to make out some of their special features: the juicy green bodies standing on six thin dark legs; the two dark eyes set wide apart on their heads; the two feelers which for the moment are swept back over their bodies; the two tubes rising sharply from the rear like protecting cannons.

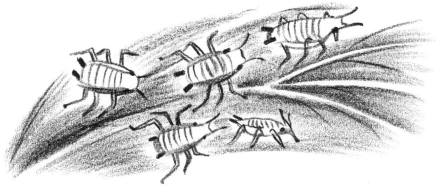

THE SAP SUCKERS

Be prepared to spend some time in this green world, because you will want to find out about the strange lives that these insects lead. You should not have too much trouble in finding aphids for they make many plants their homes, in gardens and fields, in orchards and forests. Begin by studying the insects right on the plant on which you find them. After finishing your outdoor study, cut off a piece of the lice-infested plant, place it in a covered jar, and take it home. Look at it from day to day.

Just what are these green bugs doing on the leaf? Study a few of them to find the answer. Turn the leaf to see the aphids from different angles. A side view will show a most important tool of these insects—a sap-sucking tube. Do you see this green beak, tipped with black, sticking into the leaf? Disturb the aphid, and watch it

SAP-SUCKING TUBE

WHEN DISTURBED, THE APHID FOLDS BACK THE TUBE AND GUIDES ITSELF WITH ITS FEELERS pull its beak out. Then it moves slowly away on its long thin legs, folding its beak under its "chest," and feeling its way along with its feelers. Finding a new spot, the aphid drills a well for itself, with a funny wigwagging of its body. The feelers are folded back again and the plant louse settles down for a long drink at its green plant fountain.

All of these creatures are busy drinking green sap and getting bigger and greener. As they get bigger they split out of their skins, having first grown a new one underneath. You will find many of these dried white skins where they were shed on the leaf by the aphids.

ANT HERDSMEN AND APHID COWS

Perhaps those who are most interested in these sap-sucking insects are the ants. You may have noticed some active ants in this quiet green world of the aphids. It is likely that these ants are milking their "cows," the aphids. Watching an ant closely, you may see it touch its antennae to the back of an aphid. The aphid then sends out a drop of liquid from the end of its food tube,

which the ant quickly laps up. This "milk" of the aphid is called *honeydew*. It is a sweetish drink made by the aphids from the sap that they suck. In return for this milk, many of these ant herdsmen take good care of their aphid cows. Some of them give battle to the enemies of the aphids. Some store and protect the aphid eggs. Some ants build special stables of mud on the plants so that the aphids that are housed in them can feed in safety.

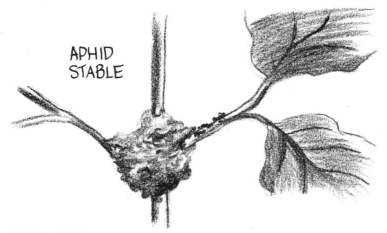

APHID STABLE

BORN ALIVE

"Where do all these aphids come from?" you ask as your lens shows leaf after leaf covered with them. To find the answer, we must understand something of the strange ways in which aphids reproduce more aphids. A little experiment will help. Find a large aphid and place it on a piece of paper on a table. Crush it gently with a pencil. First you will see a thin green liquid come out. This is the plant sap. You will also see some

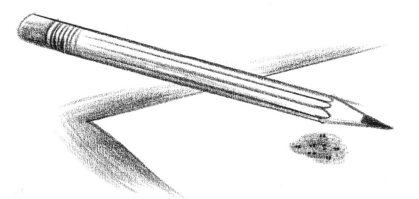

moist greenish stuff. Looking closely with your lens, you see many black dots scattered in this green mass. These are the eyes of the unborn baby aphids, and the green stuff is their bodies. Divide the number of dots by two and you will have the number of baby aphids that were inside the mother. There are usually about ten. Aphids are different from most other insects in that many of them give birth to active, living young instead of laying eggs.

A RAPID MULTIPLICATION SYSTEM

In the insect world, ten babies at a time isn't many. But there is more to the story. Ten days after the babies are born, they are having their own babies! You can prove this to yourself by crushing a small aphid. There is a very good chance that you will find unborn aphids inside.

Let's look at the arithmetic of this rapid multiplication system. Begin with one aphid, just born. Ten days later, we have ten new aphids. Ten days later, one hundred are born. Ten days after that, a thousand. One thousand

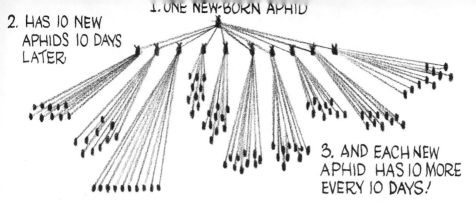

2. HAS 10 NEW
APHIDS 10 DAYS
LATER

3. AND EACH NEW
APHID HAS 10 MORE
EVERY 10 DAYS!

from one in one month! But we haven't counted the 111 parents (1 plus 10 plus 100) who might still be around. And we haven't counted those aphids who gave birth to a second and a third and a fourth batch of children.

When life becomes too crowded on the home plant, some of the aphids grow wings and fly off to start a new colony on another plant. You may have seen some of these winged aphids on the plant that you studied.

A FEMALE'S WORLD

Let us go back for a moment to our aphid arithmetic. Haven't we made a mistake in our figures by taking it for granted that all the aphids are females? No, because they are. All of the aphids born during most of the spring are females. No males are needed. Each female aphid produces more female aphids.

When the cold weather sets in, however, males as well as females appear in the aphid families. These end-of-the-season aphids mate, male with female, to produce special eggs called *winter eggs*. These eggs are laid in the cracks of bark or on the lower ends of branches and buds. The parents die in the cold of winter but the eggs live. They will hatch out the following spring to start a new colony of female aphids.

APHID ENEMIES

Why haven't these rapid reproducers eaten up all the plant life in the world? One good reason is that aphids make a juicy meal for many of their insect enemies. One of these is the aphis lion, which is the name given to the young stage of the fly called lacewing. The aphis lion has two long curved jaws, which are really hollow sucking tubes. When the lion captures an aphid it lifts it right off its feet and promptly sucks it dry. In this way, the thirsty lions may kill an average of ten aphids a day.

APHID ENEMIES

APHIS LION

LADYBUG

Another enemy of the aphids is the familiar beetle called the ladybird. Against these, the weak aphids have very little defense, although some scientists who have studied aphids carefully report that they have seen the aphids squeeze some wax out of their two rear tubes and smear it into the jaws and mouth of the attacking insects. While the attacker is trying to clean itself, the aphid escapes.

Another enemy cannot be met in this way. You will find the remains of its work in the empty brown aphid shells, each with a little round door cut out of it. This inside job is done by a four-winged "fly" which lays its eggs inside the green living aphid. The eggs grow into small, wormlike creatures which eat their way out of the aphid, leaving only the dried shell, with its neat little door.

WHO WILL WIN?

Man is high in the list of aphid enemies. He has good reason to be. Aphids weaken or kill many plants that are valuable to man. Just to give one example: in 1944, in the northern states of our country, aphids caused a loss of 66½ million dollars in the potato crop.

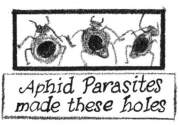

Aphid Parasites made these holes

Aphids cause damage not only by sucking sap but also by carrying disease germs from plant to plant. These germs, called viruses, do a great deal of damage to potatoes, peas, beans, melons, strawberries, orange trees, and many other plants.

Man uses chemicals in his warfare against his insect enemies. One of these chemicals is DDT. Try a little of this warfare yourself by spraying your aphid-infested plant, in its jar, with DDT. Look at the results the next day to see how the DDT worked. You will find that the green bodies have turned brown, many of them still in the same feeding position that they died in, with their beaks in the leaves.

The struggle between man and the aphid is going on today. These little drops of "sap on legs," with their rapid multiplication system, stand up against man with his chemical warfare and his armies of insect allies. Who will win? Probably neither. Man will probably never get rid of all of these pests, but he will be able to hold them in check.

A Hundred Pearls

A HUNDRED GLISTENING PEARLS wrapped in the finest silk. This tempting treasure may be no farther away from you than the nearest spider web. You may have to hunt in dark, unused places—under the porch or on the attic walls —for these spider homes. But the only equipment you need is a covered jar and the courage to come close to spiders and webs.

A SACK OF EGGS

Hanging in some of these cobwebs may be the object of your search— little gray-brown sacs. Don't be surprised if you also see a spider lurking nearby. To capture both at once, hold the open jar under them. Then use the lid to push them in and to close the jar. When you are ready to look at your treasure, take the brown sac out of a jar. Line a small container (a matchbox is good) with some dark-colored paper. Now, holding the sac over the box, carefully pull the silken threads from two opposite sides.

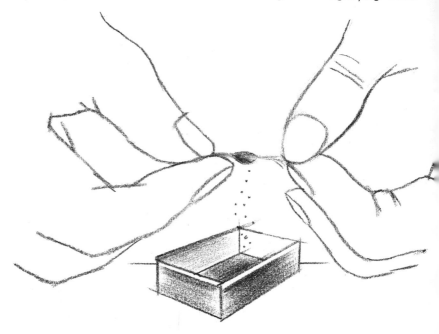

A shower of tiny specks begins to fall into the box. To see the treasure, the many perfect, glistening pearls, look at these specks under a bright light with your magnifying glass. You have, of course, just opened the egg sac of the spider. Each of the "pearls" is really a spider egg. How many eggs are there in your sac? A hundred is about average, but you may have as few as fifty or as many as two hundred. How big are these eggs? Use your lens to help you find the answer. While looking through it, use a needle to line the eggs up in a single file along the inside edge of the box. Your magnifying glass shows you that just about fifty of them fit com-

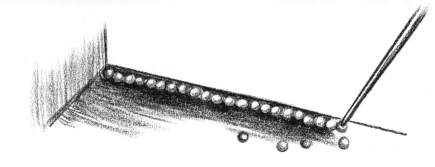

fortably in one inch. Perhaps you have found young spiders in the sac instead of eggs. This is not surprising, since the quick-growing spiders spend some time in the egg sac before they crawl out. Instead of the bouncy, pearly eggs, your magnifying glass shows you a sea of delicately moving legs, with spider bodies attached. But whether you find eggs or spiderlings, you can watch them grow day by day by keeping them in a dark, covered box in a cool place. You can feed your spiderlings small, living insects like ants or aphids.

THE SPIDER AND THE FLY

At the same time, give some of your attention to the mother spider whom you left in the jar. Place a twig in the jar to make it easy for her to attach the silken threads for her new web. With the help of your magnifying glass, you are in a good position to watch the spider making her silk from the fingerlike spinnerets that are found near the end of her body. Watch this engineer build her cobweb in your bottle. If you want some

special excitement, place a small living insect like an ant or a fly in the jar. Watch the show with a large, low-powered magnifying glass. First see the insect get tangled in the threads of the cobweb. Then watch the spider, which until now has been hanging with its feet all crumpled up around its body, awake into real action. Darting close to its victim, it uses its hind legs to throw some freshly made silk around it. The insect is now in a pretty helpless condition, but the spider darts back anyway. A few moments later it ties some more silken threads around the insect. Finally it kills its prey and sucks the juices out of it.

ALL KINDS OF CASES

If you are lucky you may be able to see how the spider makes her egg case. First she spins a silken sheet from some special silk that she makes. She then lays the eggs, one by one, from an opening near the end of her body. After all the eggs are laid, the spider finishes the making of the silken sac.

Spider egg cases come in many sizes and shapes. The egg sac of the house spider is in the form of a little ball. The common garden spider makes a pear-shaped egg sac which is as large as a hickory nut. Some egg sacs are in the form of flat, papery, silvery disks, which you may find attached to stones or to wooden or concrete structures.

SOME HANG IN WEBS

SOME ARE LIKE FUZZY BALLS

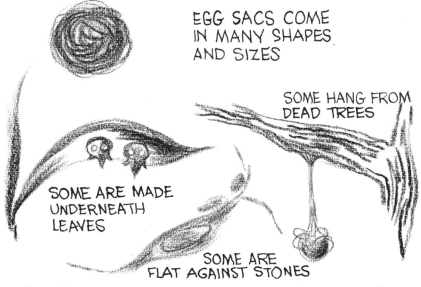

EGG SACS COME IN MANY SHAPES AND SIZES

SOME HANG FROM DEAD TREES

SOME ARE MADE UNDERNEATH LEAVES

SOME ARE FLAT AGAINST STONES

The silken covering is made to protect the eggs and the spiderlings from their enemies, particuarly insects. The sacs of some spiders have a very thin silken covering, but even this is enough to tangle up any insect that might try to get through. Some sacs are well protected, being made of two or three thick layers of silk. Some spider sacs are plastered with mud. Others are camouflaged with tiny bits of wood, leaves, or stone to make them look like their surroundings. In this way they are not noticed by their enemies.

SAC

The spiderlings of the house spider hatch out of the eggs one week after they are laid. At first they feed on each other inside the sac. (Don't be surprised if the number of spiderlings in your box seems to get smaller, day by day.) Later, crawling out of the sac, the young spiderlings feed on scraps they find in their mothers' nests. At last they leave to build their own webs, catch their own food, and, some day, to make their own silken sacs filled with pearly eggs.

SPIDERLINGS CRAWL OUT OF THE SAC

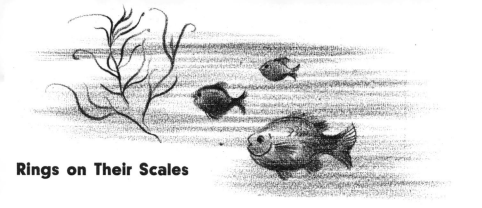

Rings on Their Scales

How MANY YEARS DOES IT TAKE the bluegill (which we often call the sunfish) to grow to a length of 6 inches? This is the kind of question which interests the scientists who are trying to keep our lakes and streams well stocked with fish. To find the answer, they trapped hundreds of 6-inch bluegills. They found that most of them were in the fourth summer of their lives. Just how could they tell the age of these fish?

COLLECTING FISH SCALES

Most people know that the age of a tree can be found by counting its yearly growth rings. Not many, however, know that fish have growth rings too, on every scale of their bodies. You can see these rings, and some very interesting designs at the same time, by making your own collection of dried fish scales. Your neighborhood fish dealer will probably be glad to supply you with some of the scales which he scrapes off the fish when he cleans

TREE TRUNKS HAVE YEARLY GROWTH RINGS

SO DO FISH SCALES

them for his customers. Visit him some morning equipped with a batch of envelopes. Write the names of the fish that he has on sale that day, one on each envelope. Your fish dealer will fill the envelopes for you.

When you get the scales home, you will probably want to clean and dry them. These dried fish scales will keep for years. If they curl at the edges, you can flatten them out for study by soaking them in water. In a short time, with the aid of your fish dealer and your fishing friends, you can build up an interesting collection of many kinds of fish scales.

SEA BASS

SEA ROBIN

PORGIE

SALMON

FLOUNDER

RINGS

Experiment with different kinds of lighting when looking at the scales. Try placing them on a dark surface, under a strong light. Also try looking through the scales at a light. Whichever method you use, you will be surprised at their many interesting shapes and their detailed designs. The scales of some fish look like scallop shells and others like shields; some are like bells and others are like tiles; some are round and others are oval. Some scales have many tiny spines at one end. Some have ribs, but all are etched with many fine lines or rings.

THE RINGS LOOK
DARK AGAINST A
LIGHT BACKGROUND

AND LIGHT AGAINST
A DARK BACKGROUND

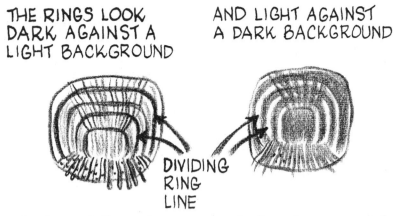

DIVIDING
RING
LINE

Look carefully at these rings, which make a series of circles around the scale, something like the growth rings on a tree. Do you see that some of the rings seem to stand out from the others, dividing the scale into a number of wide bands? These dividing lines look white if you are looking at the scale on a dark background, or dark if you are looking through the scale at a light.

3-D

To see these lines more clearly and to witness a wonderful color show at the same time, look at the scales with polarized light. The only new thing that you will need for this are two pieces of polarized plastic. You will find these in the "eyeglasses" that are given away at showings of three-dimensional moving pictures. Cut a pair of these in half across the cardboard bridge. Place

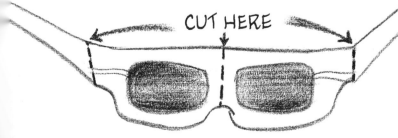

CUT HERE

a few of the scales on one of these plastic lenses. Hold it over a bright light. Place the other lens over it, turning it until a purple-blue color appears. At this time you will see that the scales gleam in many colors. A breathtaking scene awaits you when you use your magnifying on these gleaming scales. The lines stand out clearly; beautiful colors light up the ribs and rings of the scale, giving it a three-dimensional appearance.

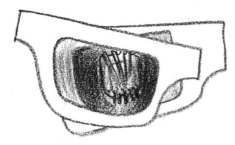

HOLD FISH SCALE "SANDWICH" BETWEEN THE LIGHT AND YOUR GLASS

PUT SCALE BETWEEN LENSES, TURN TO PURPLE POSITION

YEAR MARKS

What accounts for the many fine rings and the fewer dividing lines? First let us talk about the rings. Each of these is a growth ring. As the fish grows, its scales grow. Ring after ring of bony material is added to each of its scales. The outermost rings are those which have just been added, while those in the center are the oldest. Unlike a tree, however, many of these fine rings are made in one year.

FISH GROW FASTER IN WARM WEATHER, WHEN THERE IS PLENTY OF FOOD

To understand how the dividing lines are made we must understand that a fish does not grow steadily throughout the year. In the warmer months, when food is plentiful, growth is rapid. On its scales this fast growth results in many evenly spaced rings. In the colder months, the fish grows very slowly, if at all. Its growth rings are few and close together. It is these winter rings that you saw as a light or dark dividing line.

Actually, then, each of these winter lines marks the end of a year's growth. To find the age of a fish, we count the number of these year marks. Try to find the age of each kind of fish for which you have scales. You will find this easy for some, quite hard for others.

READING RING STORIES

But scales can tell us more than the age of a fish—if we know how to read their stories. Look, for example, at the scale of this rock bass, which lived in Booth Lake. Counting its year marks, we know that it is four years old. Notice also that the summer growth band between its third and fourth winter is much broader than those of other years. The scale has grown almost as much in its fourth year as in its first three years together. And so has the whole fish. How can we account for this spurt in the fourth year?

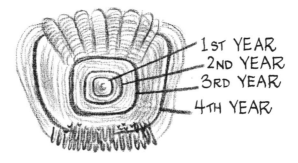

1st YEAR
2nd YEAR
3rd YEAR
4th YEAR

The game warden has the answer. He tells us that at a time when this bass was three years old, he trapped and removed many of the fish of Booth Lake. The remaining bass were able to get more food than they had had in past seasons. As a result they grew larger and heavier.

Here, then, is one example of how the study of these age-telling, growth-measuring scales helps those whose job it is to see to it that our fishing waters are well stocked with good-sized fish.

Designed by Man

THE
LETTERS
ARE HERE

Hidden Letters

DID YOU KNOW that your Lincoln penny has some hidden letters on it? These letters, which most people never see, are so carefully hidden that you would have to look for hours unless you were told where they were. Any Lincoln penny from 1918 on has these letters, but you will do best to look for them on a new or unused penny. The letters are hidden under Lincoln's shoulder. To find them use your magnifying glass under a good light and tilt the penny away from you.

VDB

The hidden letters are VDB. Why are they there? These letters are the initials of Victor D. Brenner, the artist who designed the Lincoln penny. This penny first appeared in 1909 to celebrate the one hundredth anniversary of Lincoln's birth. At that time the artist's initials were very clearly shown on the back of the coin. In fact, many people felt that they were much too big and that they attracted too much attention. As a result, the pennies minted later in 1909 did not have his initials at all, nor did any pennies until 1918. In that year Brenner's initials were put back on the penny in the hidden place where you found it.

THE INITIAL IS
HERE

The old Indian-head penny also has a hidden letter on it. If you have one in good condition, you will be able to find the initial L on the bonnet ribbon of the Indian girl. To see it, turn the coin slightly so that the girl faces you and look for the L under a good light with your magnifying glass. This letter, the initial of the designer Longacre, appeared on all Indian-head pennies from 1864 until 1909, the last year in which this penny was minted.

NICKELS, DIMES, AND QUARTERS

On most of the coins that are in circulation today, there are the initials of the designers, usually very tiny and often hidden. Let us look for some. The Indian-head or Buffalo nickel, which was minted between 1913 and 1938, was designed by James E. Fraser whose initial F you can find cut into the coin under the date. The artist used real Indians as models for the face of the coin. The bison on the other side was modeled after "Black Diamond," who was in the New York Zoo.

"BLACK DIAMOND"
WAS THE MODEL

The Winged Victory dime was designed by A. A. Weinman. You will find the raised monogram of the designer, a combined A and W, to the right of Liberty's neck. This dime is often called the Mercury dime, after the Roman god. The artist, however, intended that the wings crowning the figure's head stand for freedom of thought. This coin had a run between 1916 and 1945.

The Roosevelt dime which followed it was designed by John R. Sinnock and appeared in 1946. You can find the raised JS to the left of the date and under the neck of Roosevelt. This coin has a simple, modern design.

The Standing Liberty quarter, which had a run from 1916 until 1930, was designed by Herman A. MacNeil. You will find an M cut into the coin to the right of Liberty's feet. The Washington quarter which followed it has the artist's initials hidden in the same way as on the Lincoln penny. You will find JF for the designer, John Flanagan, by tilting the coin away from you. This quarter appeared in 1932 to celebrate the two hundredth anniversary of Washington's birth.

THE SAN FRANCISCO MINT

PHILADELPHIA, DENVER, AND SAN FRANCISCO

You may have noticed the letter D or S on some coins. These letters stand for Denver and San Francisco, the places where the coins were made. Coins which do not have any mark at all were minted in Philadelphia. Here are the mint marks on some coins:

(VERY LARGE INITIAL ON SOME JEFFERSON NICKELS)

Since the number of coins minted in Denver, San Francisco, and other branch mints of the past has been much less than the coinage at Philadelphia, these coins are scarcer. This makes them more valuable to coin collectors.

MAKING METAL MONEY

Coins are made by striking blank pieces of metal with a mold having a design on it. The blank is held tightly by a collar as it is struck from above and below at the same time. The power of the blow is great, ranging from 40 tons for a penny to 170 tons for a silver dollar. If you look at the edge of any silver coin, you will see that there are many little lines on it. This *reeding*, as it is called, is made by having grooves in the collar we just spoke about. The blow forces the coin into the grooves and gives it the reeding.

There are two reasons why coins are reeded. One is that it is harder to counterfeit the coin. Another, and probably more important, reason is that it prevents dishonest people from shaving the silver off the edge of coins in order to rob the government of this precious metal.

COINING PRESS

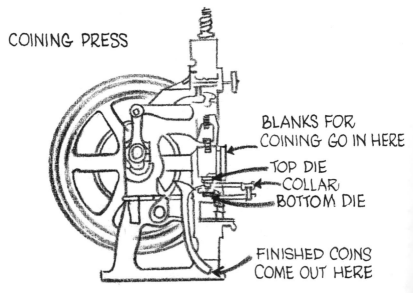

BLANKS FOR COINING GO IN HERE

TOP DIE

COLLAR

BOTTOM DIE

FINISHED COINS COME OUT HERE

Counterfeit coins can be detected in three ways:

1. Look. Look at the edge. In a good coin the reeding lines are even and they are spaced regularly. In bad coins the lines are crooked, unevenly spaced, and sometimes missing.

2. Listen. Bounce the coin on a hard surface. It should ring in clear, bell-like tones. Counterfeit coins sound dull.

3. Feel. Counterfeit coins have a greasy feel.

DESIGN ON PAPER

It certainly is hard for a counterfeiter to make a copy of our paper money. Look at a one-dollar bill with your magnifying glass. What a richness of detailed design! Scrolls, crosslines, curlicues, and fish-net patterns; care-fully counted stars and arrows; the delicately etched fea-

Published by Special Permission of Chief, U. S. Secret Service, Treasury Dept. Further reproduction, in whole or part, is strictly prohibited

tures of Washington, with his lifelike eyes; the fine red and blue silken threads, woven right into the fabric of the paper; the carefully designed figures in the seals.

Turn your lens on the great seal of the Treasury. This seal, which is blue on the one-dollar bill, is older than the Constitution of the United States. On the white shield of this seal are the balanced scales of justice. Lower down on the shield is a key. You might think of this as the key to the treasury, rightfully held by the Treasury Department. In the blue band above the key are thirteen white stars, which stand for the thirteen original states of our country.

THE GREAT SEAL OF
THE TREASURY

OUR LUCKY NUMBER

Thirteen was our country's lucky number! You will find the thirteen states represented in other parts of the bill. Turn to the back of the dollar to see the mysterious-looking Great Seal of the United States. The pyramid has thirteen steps or bars on it. Above the pyramid is an eye in a triangle. On the right side of the bill is the other side of the Great Seal. The eagle there has thirteen arrows clasped in its left claw. Above the eagle is a design with thirteen stars in it. See if you can find any other combinations of thirteen on the bill.

ENGRAVERS WITH MAGNIFYING GLASSES

All of these tiny details that you have found on our paper money were made originally by the hands of men working on steel plates. How is it possible for these men, called *engravers*, to make details that are so fine that it takes a magnifying glass to find them? The answer is that the engravers, too, use a magnifying glass when they work. While looking through a powerful lens, they cut into a steel plate with a fine, sharp tool called a *graver*.

Many men work on the engraving of the plates for one type of bill. Some give all their time to the lettering, some to the details of the portrait, some to the scrolls. The engravers must be very careful about every line that they cut into the steel. The slightest slip could spoil the work of months. No counterfeiter has ever duplicated the artistic work of the expert engravers of our Bureau of Engraving and Printing.

KNOW YOUR MONEY

All of this work is needed to make a perfectly designed bill and one that is hard to counterfeit. But, as you know, counterfeit bills are made. The United States Secret Service, in a pamphlet called "Know Your Money"

tells how to know good money from bad. We are advised to examine the details of the portrait carefully. On counterfeit money the picture is dull and smudgy, and it does not stand out clearly from the dark background. On good bills the picture stands out clearly and the eyes are lifelike.

On the colored seal which you saw before, the saw-toothed points on bad bills are usually uneven and some of them may be broken off. On good bills, the saw-toothed points are even and sharp. The serial numbers on counterfeit bills are poorly printed and badly spaced. In general, the fine lines of a good bill are clear and even, while those of a bad bill are broken and ragged.

In its work in detecting bad bills, the Treasury Department uses magnifying glasses and powerful microscopes to find flaws in the design and in the printing. You, with your magnifying glass, can be an agent of the Treasury, and at the same time protect yourself by being on the lookout for counterfeit money.

THESE THINGS ARE WRONG ON COUNTERFEIT BILLS

PORTRAITS ARE DULL AND SMUDGY

POINTS ON THE SEAL ARE UNEVEN AND BROKEN

S34 11

SERIAL NUMBERS ARE BADLY PRINTED AND SPACED

Pictures from Dots

THE PICTURES THAT YOU SEE in newspapers and magazines are made entirely from dots, as you can easily prove to yourself with a magnifying glass. Begin with a photograph in your daily newspaper. Look at the whitest part of it with your lens. You will find that there are many little black dots in it, evenly spaced from one another. Just how many dots are there? To find out, rule a line ¼ inch long on the white area and count the num-

RULE A LINE ¼" LONG
ON THE WHITEST SPACE

ber of dots along it. Since printers usually count by the inch, multiply your answer by four. You will probably find that there are about 65 dots to the inch. This means that there are 65 times 65 or 4,225 dots in every square inch of the picture.

LIGHTEST AREA

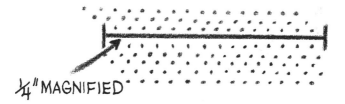

¼" MAGNIFIED

FROM GRAY TO BLACK

Turn your lens now on a gray part of the photograph. You will find that the number of dots is exactly the same. The spacing is the same. The blackness of the ink is the same. Then what makes it look different from the white area? Your lens shows you that the dots are larger in this gray area. Without the lens, you cannot see the dots, or the spaces between them. The black dots and the white space are mixed to make an even gray tone.

IN A GRAYER AREA, THE DOTS ARE LARGER

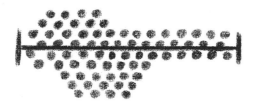

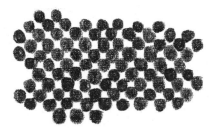

In a slightly grayer part of the picture, you discover that the dots are still larger. They are quite square now; the whole pattern looks like a checkerboard. Half of the paper is white and half is covered with ink.

In a dark gray area, the black parts of the checkerboard have run together to cover more than half of the paper. Now the white, unprinted part of the paper appears as dots, standing out against the black background. In the gray-black and jet-black areas the white dots become smaller, practically disappearing.

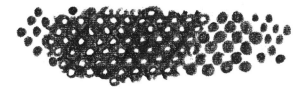

The magnifying glass has shown us that the whole picture, even parts that look like lines and parts that look pure white, is made of black dots. It has shown us that the range of tones from white to black is made by increasing the size of the dots.

MORE DOTS TO THE INCH

YOU CAN'T MAKE AS DETAILED A PICTURE

Why do the photographs in many magazines look clearer than those in the daily newspaper? To find the answer, look at a black and white picture in any of the popular weekly magazines. Under the magnifying glass you find that these pictures have more dots to the inch, perhaps 80 or more. This means that there are 6,400 dots to the square inch. With more dots to work with, the printer can show the details in a picture more clearly, just as you could make a sharper, more detailed picture with a fine pencil than with a thick crayon.

WITH A CRAYON

AS YOU CAN WITH A SHARP PENCIL

Then why don't the newspapers use more dots to get finer pictures? For the same reason that you would prefer to use a thick crayon rather than a fine pencil to write on a rough piece of cardboard. Newspapers are printed on rough, uneven paper. The larger dots print better on the hills and valleys of this paper. For this reason, newspapers are usually printed with not more than 65 dots to the inch. Finer bond papers can take 85 to 100 dots. The best papers can take 120 dots and up.

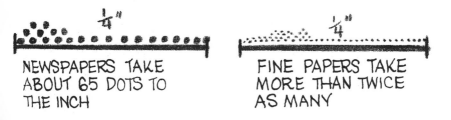

NEWSPAPERS TAKE ABOUT 65 DOTS TO THE INCH

FINE PAPERS TAKE MORE THAN TWICE AS MANY

A SPRINKLING OF COLORED DOTS

How are the color pictures in magazines made? Under the magnifying glass, you discover that color pictures, like black and white ones, are made of dots. At first glance you see an interesting honeycomb pattern made by the many groups of dots. As you continue to look, you see that there are dots of different colors in each of these groups. Most magazines use blue, red, and yellow dots, and some have black dots in addition.

With the lens you discover that the lovely flesh tones of the moving-picture actress on the cover of the magazine are made of large yellow and red dots and much smaller blue ones. Her pearly white teeth are made of small red, yellow, and blue dots, with a good deal of empty white in between. The brown pair of slacks of the man in the advertisement is made of large red and yellow dots and smaller black ones.

The printer, by sprinkling these differently colored dots across the page, can make many different colors. This is something like mixing paints to get the color you want, except that in this case the colors are not mixed on the paper. It is your eye, which cannot separate these differently colored dots, that really does the mixing to get the blended colors.

FROM LINES TO DOTS

Printers call pictures made from dots *halftones*. Before we knew how to make halftones, all the pictures that appeared in newspapers and magazines were printed from woodcuts or from line drawings, like this picture of Lincoln that appeared in a newspaper shortly after his death. Although photography was fairly well developed

at that time, there was no way of printing a photograph on a newspaper press. Before 1900, however, two men, Frederick E. Ives and Max Levy, discovered that photographs could be printed on a press if they were first broken up into many small dots. This was done by photographing the photograph through a screen. In the printing plate that was finally made from this picture, each dot became a raised peak which could pick up ink and press it on white paper.

THE HALFTONE SCREEN FITS INTO THE CAMERA BETWEEN THE NEGATIVE AND THE LENS

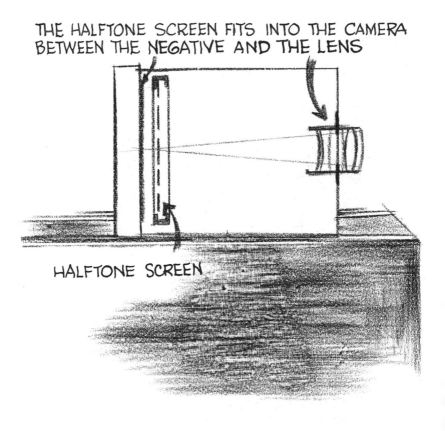

HALFTONE SCREEN

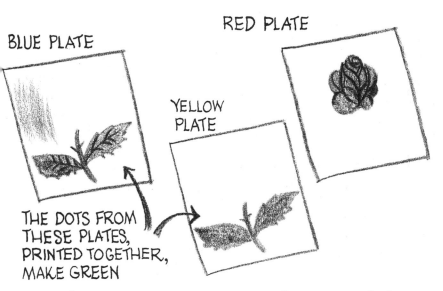

BLUE PLATE

RED PLATE

YELLOW PLATE

THE DOTS FROM THESE PLATES, PRINTED TOGETHER, MAKE GREEN

In color printing, separate printing plates are made for each of the colors. This means that the paper gets its red color from one plate, its blue from a second, and its yellow from a third. In one kind of color printing, the colors fall directly on top of each other. In another, like the kind that you probably saw in the magazine picture, the plates are so made that the differently colored dots fall side by side, and not on top of each other.

The discovery of how to change a picture taken with a camera or painted by an artist into a pattern of raised dots on a printing plate has made it possible to reach millions of people quickly and easily with true copies of the original.

Seeing Sound

WHAT DOES A HIGH NOTE look like? What does a low note look like? You can find the answer in the grooves of a phonograph record if you use your eyes instead of your ears. There you will see the stored music of jazz or symphony, of folk song or opera.

Use the kind of record that is made to play at the speed of 78 turns a minute. Later you will find out why this kind is better for the study of grooves than the long-playing records. And since you are going to experiment with the record, use one that is not too precious to you or your family.

Lighting is important. There are many annoying and confusing reflections in a phonograph record. To get good light, sit facing a window. Tilt the record slightly away from you. If you find it hard to get good lighting, or if your magnifying glass does not seem to be powerful enough, make a print of the record. You can do this by pressing a flat, smooth piece of modeling clay against the record. Of course, the clay print is really a negative of the record. This means that there are grooves in your clay where there were ridges in your record, and ridges where there were grooves.

WRIGGLING WAVES

Either way, on the record or in its clay print, the magnifying glass shows that the grooves are not smooth lines but wriggling waves. Some of these waves are long and some are short. Some are high and some are low.

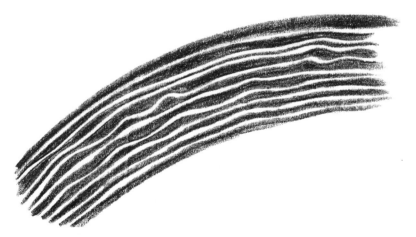

To see the waves more clearly, try running the point of a fine sewing needle along a groove in a record while looking at it through the magnifying glass. You will find that the track that the needle travels in is very narrow.

If you take the trouble to count them, you will find that there are 143 grooves lying side by side for every inch. With a little arithmetic, you can figure out that the length of the whole spiraling track on a record that plays for about five minutes is over six hundred feet.

THE TRACK IS OVER
600 FEET LONG

FROM CURVES TO MUSIC

Of course you know how to change these wriggling curves into music that fills the room—you simply turn your record player on. This time, however, do it differently. Hold a phonograph needle tightly between two fingers and let it ride in the grooves of a turning record. Do you hear the music? You can improve the results by sticking the needle through a card. Hold the card in your hand while the needle is riding in the turning record. This time the tones are louder and clearer.

Just how do curves in a record become sounds to you? As the record spins under the needle, the curves in it shake the needle in the same way that a very curvy railroad track might shake a fast-moving train. This shaking or vibration is passed along from the needle to the card. The vibrating card hits many of the invisible air molecules which happen to be near it. The air molecules pass the bounce along to one another, finally striking your eardrum. The vibration then passes through the connecting bones of your middle ear to your inner ear. Here the sound vibrations excite some nerves. The nerves then send a nerve message (not a vibration) to the brain. Here you finally hear it as sound.

5. THE NERVES THERE SEND A MESSAGE TO YOUR BRAIN. *THEN* YOU HEAR THE MUSIC.

4. THE JIGGLING AIR MOLECULES HIT YOUR EARDRUM, WHICH VIBRATES YOUR MIDDLE EAR.

3. THE VIBRATING CARD JIGGLES THE AIR MOLECULES AROUND IT

2. THE NEEDLE SHAKES THE CARD

1. THE CURVES IN THE RECORD HIT THE NEEDLE

HIGH TONE, LOW TONE

How do the waves make high-pitched tones and low-pitched tones? Look at your record, or its clay print, more closely to see the short waves looking like this:

and the long waves looking like this:

What do each of these kinds of wave tracks do to the needle that passes over them? To find the answer do a simple experiment with a pocket comb which has both fine and coarse teeth in it. Run the corner of a card over the teeth. First try the card on the fine teeth and listen. Then, with your hand moving at the same speed, run it over the coarse teeth. Try this a number of times. Hum the notes that you hear.

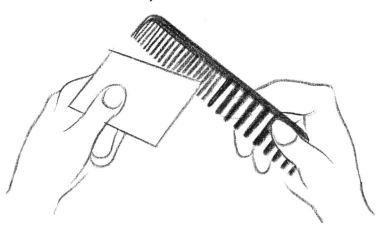

You will find that the card buzzes in a high pitch when it runs over the fine teeth, and in a lower pitch when it runs over the coarse teeth. You will also notice that the card gets more bumps as it passes over the fine teeth. This is not surprising since there are twice as many fine teeth as there are coarse ones. And the more bumps the card gets, the faster it shakes.

We get a high pitch, then, when the card shakes quickly. We get a low pitch when the card shakes slowly. The same is true in a phonograph. The short waves shake the needle rapidly to make the high-pitched tones. The long waves shake the needle slowly to make the low tones.

QUICK SHAKES MAKE A HIGH PITCH

SLOWER SHAKES ARE LOW TONES

TALL WAVES MAKE LOUD TONES

SHALLOW WAVES MAKE SOFT TONES

Although they are very difficult to see with a magnifying glass, there are differences in the *heights* as well as the length of the waves. The tall waves make the loud tones and the shallow waves make the soft tones.

CUTTING A GROOVE

When we *play* a record, we are changing the waves in a flat disk into air waves which travel to our ears. In the *making* of a record we do just the opposite; we change air waves into record waves.

Vibrating vocal cords in our throats or vibrating strings in a violin start the air quivering. These sound waves are picked up by the diaphragm in a microphone and changed into electric waves. These electric waves cause an electromagnet to vibrate the recording needle. The needle cuts a wavy track in a turning wax disk. The records that we buy are exact copies, in hardened shellac or plastic, of the original wax recording.

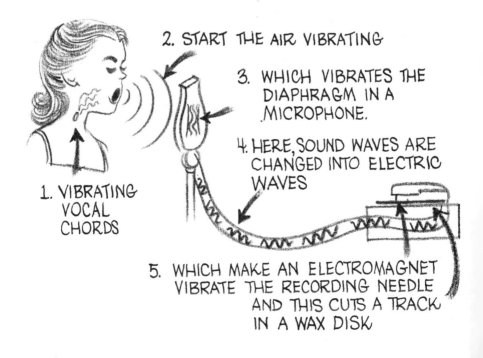

2. START THE AIR VIBRATING

3. WHICH VIBRATES THE DIAPHRAGM IN A MICROPHONE.

4. HERE, SOUND WAVES ARE CHANGED INTO ELECTRIC WAVES

1. VIBRATING VOCAL CHORDS

5. WHICH MAKE AN ELECTROMAGNET VIBRATE THE RECORDING NEEDLE AND THIS CUTS A TRACK IN A WAX DISK

LP

How is it possible for the long-playing records to play for as long as thirty minutes? A quick look at one of the records through the magnifying glass gives the answer. Everything is smaller; so more music can be cut into the record. Since the waves are smaller, the records can be played more slowly (33 or 45 turns a minute) and yet give the true notes. Since the grooves are narrower, more of them can be cut on one record. With slower speed and a longer track, these records can play for half an hour without a break in the music.

A LASTING RECORD

Ever since man invented the tom-tom, he has known that he could make sound come out of objects by banging them. For many centuries he has known that this banging started a vibration which traveled to the human ear to be sensed as sound. It was only one step more to learn how to trap and store these vibrations in a soft, plastic material to make a lasting record.

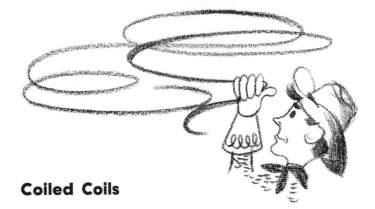

Coiled Coils

HELP WANTED

SOMETHING that carries electricity; stretches into a wire finer than a hair, but does not break; heats to 5,000 or 6,000 degrees Fahrenheit, but does not melt; glows with a brilliant white light when hot.

THIS WAS THE KIND OF SUBSTANCE that was wanted by the scientists who were trying to improve the old Edison electric bulb. They wanted something to take the place of the long carbon threads, the filaments, in these bulbs. True, these carbon filaments had served well in their job of glowing brightly when electricity was passed through them. But carbon had one serious disadvantage: when it became hot, small particles from it would fly off and coat the inside of the bulb. The bulb became dimmer and the filament became thinner. Finally the filament would break, ending the life of the lamp.

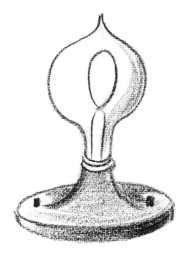

EDISON'S FIRST
ELECTRIC
LIGHT

TUNGSTEN GETS THE JOB

It took the work of many men to find that the hard, gray material, commonly called *tungsten*, could be made to do a better job. You can see the results of this work by looking at the inside of an electric bulb. Get a 100-watt bulb of clear glass so that you can look right through it.

Rising from the base of the bulb is a glass tube through which the lead-in wires pass. These wires carry the electric current from the metal contacts in the base to the filament above. On the top of the glass rod are three wire supports. Two of these keep the lead-in wires in place. The third supports the filament which is attached to the ends of the lead-in wires.

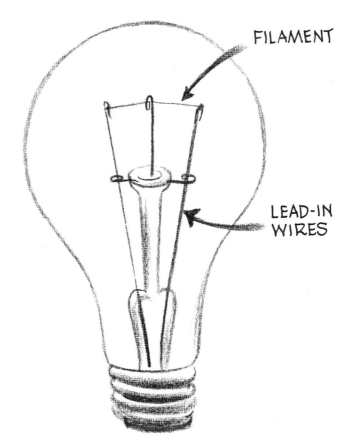

FILAMENT

LEAD-IN WIRES

1,000 LOOPLETS

Look at this tungsten filament carefully. Even without magnification, your eye tells you that this delicate wire is coiled like a spring. Now look at the coil with your magnifying glass. (If you find that you cannot get close enough with your lens to bring the filament in sharp focus, you will have to break the bulb. To do this, place the bulb in a wax-paper bag, which in turn is placed in a heavy brown bag. Break the bulb in a deep metal can, like a garbage can, by tapping it gently with a hammer. Open the bags carefully. If you are lucky, the filament may still be attached to the lead-in wires. Otherwise, look for it among the broken pieces of glass, using a pair of tweezers to help you.)

WHEN YOU BREAK THE
BULB, IT WILL PROBABLY
SHATTER. BE SURE YOU
PUT IT IN
    1. A WAX PAPER BAG
       (A SANDWICH BAG
       IS GOOD)
    2. INSIDE A BROWN
       PAPER BAG
    3. IN A DEEP
       METAL CAN
THEN
    TAP IT WITH
    THE HAMMER

TO YOUR EYE, THE FILAMENT
LOOKS LIKE THIS

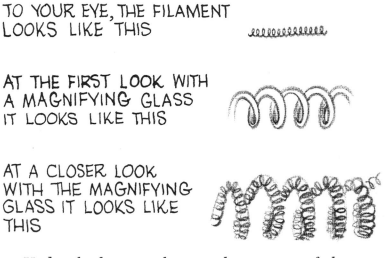

AT THE FIRST LOOK WITH
A MAGNIFYING GLASS
IT LOOKS LIKE THIS

AT A CLOSER LOOK
WITH THE MAGNIFYING
GLASS IT LOOKS LIKE
THIS

Under the lens you have a clearer view of the more than thirty carefully turned loops of the silvery gray metal, forming a perfect spiral. As you look at the loops more carefully, you discover that each of them is made of smaller loops. A powerful lens or a microscope would show that there are about thirty of these tiny looplets in each loop. That means that there are about one thousand looplets in all. If this ¾-inch filament were pulled out straight, it would be over two feet long!

HEAT AND LIGHT

Two feet of this thin tungsten wire will heat up to 4000 degrees Fahrenheit when an electric current flows through it. At this temperature it glows with a brilliant white light.

But there is another reason for packing the filament into coiled coils. The coils keep each other warm! In this way, less heat is lost from the filament. This means that more of the money that you spend for electricity goes for useful light, and less of it for wasteful heat.

NATURE'S COILS

We have seen how two feet of wire can be fitted into a small space. Nature makes use of the idea behind this in many of her own inventions. The intestines of man, for example, must be over twenty feet long to digest the food that he eats and to pass it into the blood stream. To fit the small space allotted them in the abdomen, the intestines are formed into a neat coil. The idea of the coiled coil is here also, because the inside lining of the intestine is not smooth but instead is curved into millions of tiny waves. This brings a large area of intestine lining in close touch with the food that is to be digested. There are many examples of this in nature and in manmade designs, but in all the idea seems to be—make it small and you make it large.

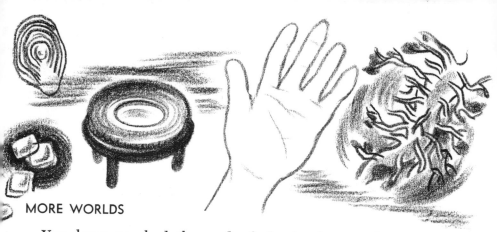

MORE WORLDS

You have reached the end of the book. You have found how this precious instrument, the magnifying glass, has opened up many wonderful sights in the world of plants and animals, and in the inventions of man himself. You have found how small details make a big difference in the way things work.

This is the end of the book, but there is no end to discovery. Use your magnifying glass to guide you in making new discoveries for yourself.

Perhaps, some day soon, you will want to use those combinations of lenses which we call microscopes, magnifying 100, 400, even 1,000 times. When you do, you will find that you are ready because you have taken the first steps into the world of tiny things with your simple magnifying glass.

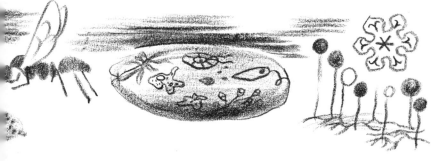

Julius Schwartz is a native New Yorker. He has taught science in the New York Public Schools for the last twenty-five years. He has also been a teacher at the City and Country School, where he set up a science program for children seven to thirteen years of age. At present he is an instructor in science education at the Bank Street College of Education.

In addition to his years of experience in teaching science, Mr. Schwartz has been an active member of the city's curriculum committees, the senior author of the booklet, *Adventures in Biology*, which is used throughout the New York City schools, the author of a great many articles for science and teaching journals, and an inspiring leader in science clubs for young people.

His book *It's Fun to Know Why* has won him a great deal of attention from children, their parents, teachers, and librarians.

Jeanne Bendick needs no introduction to readers of juvenile books. She has drawn the pictures for a great many very popular books, and she is both author and artist of such books as *All Around You, How Much and How Many*, and *Television Works Like This* (written with her husband, Robert Bendick). She and her family live on Long Island, New York.

Index